TRADE ISSUES, POLICIES AND LAWS

THE INFLUENCE OF TRADE AGREEMENTS IN GLOBAL AGRICULTURAL MARKETS

Trade Issues, Policies and Laws

Additional books in this series can be found on Nova's website under the Series tab.

Additional E-books in this series can be found on Nova's website under the E-book tab.

Agriculture Issues and Policies

Additional books in this series can be found on Nova's website under the Series tab.

Additional E-books in this series can be found on Nova's website under the E-book tab.

TRADE ISSUES, POLICIES AND LAWS

THE INFLUENCE OF TRADE AGREEMENTS IN GLOBAL AGRICULTURAL MARKETS

BENJAMIN STENTON
EDITOR

nova publishers
New York

For permission to use material from this book please contact us:
Telephone 631-231-7269; Fax 631-231-8175
Web Site: http://www.novapublishers.com

Library of Congress Cataloging-in-Publication Data

ISBN: 978-1-62417-388-2

Published by Nova Science Publishers, Inc. † New York

Contents

PREFACE

Regional and bilateral free trade agreements (FTAs) have taken on greater significance amidst an evolving international trading environment. Member countries in FTAs agree to eliminate trade barriers on all or most goods and services traded among them. Uncertainties associated with global negotiations under the World Trade Organization (WTO) Doha Development Agenda, along with other factors, have contributed to an upsurge in bilateral and regional trade agreements. This book examines the possible impacts on U.S. agricultural trade of two recently implemented FTAs in which the United States is not a partner; the FTAs between the ASEAN countries and China and between the ASEAN countries and Australia/New Zealand. Also discussed is the potential effects on U.S. agricultural exporters of pending bilateral TAs between the United States and Korea, Colombia, and Panama.

Chapter 1 - Reciprocal trade agreements (RTAs), which grant special preferences to members, affect the pattern and volume of bilateral trade in global markets. This study uses the gravity framework and panel data depicting annual trade between 69 countries over 31 years to examine how 11 RTAs have shaped U.S. and other suppliers' exports of commodity and manufactured foods. Empirical results show that joint RTA membership enabled exporters to increase their trade with member country importers in the two food markets. The few agreements that failed to have a positive effect on member trade in either commodity food or manufactured food involve developing countries that typically grant very limited cross-border trade preference to member countries. Interestingly, model results indicate that RTAs can be a vehicle to increase trade externally. Nine of the 11 RTAs also expanded exports externally to nonmember countries, albeit to a lesser degree than with member importers. In some cases, however, nonmember exporters of food bore the cost of the RTA-induced expansion of trade. Five RTAs lowered food imports from nonmember suppliers. The adverse effects on nonmember suppliers were more pronounced for the United States than for other competitors.

Chapter 2 - The rapid increase in the number of bilateral and regional free-trade agreements since 1995 is a striking development. The proliferation of these agreements has raised questions about whether they have, in fact, opened markets, created trade, promoted economic growth, and/or distorted trade. This study uses panel data from 1975 to 2005 and a gravity framework model to identify the influence of reciprocal trade agreements (RTAs) on bilateral trade in the world agricultural marketplace. A benchmark, Heckman sample-selection and two generalized models, one of which accounts for RTA phase-in effects, are used to gauge the impact on partner trade of mutual as well as asymmetric RTA membership. Empirical results show that RTAs increase agricultural trade between member countries but decrease trade between member and nonmember countries. Interestingly, RTAs were found to be particularly effective at expanding agricultural trade and opening markets in developing countries when developing-country trading partners are part of the same agreement.

Chapter 3 - Since 2001, the United States has concluded negotiations with 13 countries, resulting in 8 trade agreements (TAs). Three additional agreements have been negotiated but not yet ratified by Congress, as of March 2011. Other countries have become increasingly active in negotiating their own trade pacts. This proliferation of TAs between key U.S. trading partners and competitors may have raised concerns among U.S. exporters, whose share in established markets could be eroded by such deals. In this study, ERS examines how recently concluded TAs between ASEAN (Southeast Asia) countries and China and Australia/New Zealand, as well as pending TAs between the United States and Korea, Colombia, and Panama, will likely affect U.S. agricultural trade. Model results suggest that TAs between ASEAN countries and China and ASEAN countries and Australia/ New Zealand would result in moderate losses to U.S. agricultural exports of about $350 million to those countries, but losses would be partially offset by gains in other markets. U.S. agricultural exports to Korea would expand by an estimated $1.9 billion per year if the U.S. TA with Korea were implemented. The U.S.-Colombia TA would result in an estimated $370 million in additional U.S. exports per year. U.S. exports would realize smaller gains of about $50 million per year under the pact with Panama. Empirical results confirm theoretical findings that trade created under TAs exceeds trade diverted, but that results depend on the specific circumstances of each agreement.

In: The Influence of Trade Agreements ... ISBN: 978-1-62417-388-2
Editor: Benjamin Stenton

Chapter 1

RECIPROCAL TRADE AGREEMENTS: IMPACTS ON U.S. AND FOREIGN SUPPLIERS IN COMMODITY AND MANUFACTURED FOOD MARKETS*

Thomas Vollrath, Jason Grant and Charles Hallahan

ABSTRACT

Reciprocal trade agreements (RTAs), which grant special preferences to members, affect the pattern and volume of bilateral trade in global markets. This study uses the gravity framework and panel data depicting annual trade between 69 countries over 31 years to examine how 11 RTAs have shaped U.S. and other suppliers' exports of commodity and manufactured foods. Empirical results show that joint RTA membership enabled exporters to increase their trade with member country importers in the two food markets. The few agreements that failed to have a positive effect on member trade in either commodity food or manufactured food involve developing countries that typically grant very limited cross-border trade preference to member countries. Interestingly, model results indicate that RTAs can be a vehicle to increase trade externally. Nine of the 11 RTAs also expanded exports externally to nonmember countries, albeit to a lesser degree than with member importers. In some cases,

* This is an edited, reformatted and augmented version of United States Department of Agriculture, Economic Research Report, Number 138, dated August 2012.

however, nonmember exporters of food bore the cost of the RTA-induced expansion of trade. Five RTAs lowered food imports from nonmember suppliers. The adverse effects on nonmember suppliers were more pronounced for the United States than for other competitors.

About the Authors

Thomas Vollrath is an economist, formerly with USDA's Economic Research Service (ERS); Jason Grant is an assistant professor at Virginia Polytechnic Institute and State University; and Charles Hallahan is a research analyst with ERS.

Summary

What Is the Issue?

Reciprocal trade agreements (RTAs) between two or more countries offer an alternative approach to lower trade barriers than that provided through multilateral negotiations of the World Trade Organization (WTO). But because RTAs grant preferential cross-border treatment to member countries, they may distort markets and divert trade from nonmember exporters. This study focuses on two agricultural subsectors—commodity foods and manufactured foods—and quantifies the extent to which RTAs have expanded trade between member countries and altered trade between member and nonmember countries.

Most applied research on RTAs has examined the effects on intra-bloc trade, or trade between partners belonging to the same trading bloc. This study examines the impacts of 11 RTAs on both intra-bloc trade and extra-bloc trade, or trade between member and nonmember countries. The study also differentiates between the effects on the United States as a nonmember exporter and the effects on other nonmember competitors.

What Did the Study Find?

Given that international policy dynamics make negotiating a multilateral trade agreement difficult, countries have used RTAs as a practical and feasible route to gain greater access to foreign markets. These agreements have affected the pattern and volume of bilateral trade.

- RTA membership increased trade in most commodity and manufactured food markets during the 1975-2005 period. However, in some cases, the increase in intra-bloc trade came at the expense of a shift in imports away from nonmember food exporters.
- Not surprisingly, the rise in exports to partner markets was particularly pronounced when the exporter and the importer were members of the same RTA. For example, the formation of the European Union (EU) induced an expansion of intra-EU trade in manufactured foods and commodity foods of 93 and 95 percent, respectively, between 1975 and 2005. This growth equates to an average annual increase in food trade between EU countries of 3 percent per year.
- The rise in intra-bloc trade within the North American Free Trade Agreement (NAFTA) and the Closer Economic Relations (CER) agreement was, in contrast to that within the EU, substantially greater for manufactured foods than for commodity foods. Between 1989 and 2005, trade between NAFTA members expanded 6 percent per year, on average, in manufactured foods and 3 percent per year in commodity foods. Over the same period, trade between CER members Australia and New Zealand increased 14 percent per year in manufactured foods and 3 percent per year in commodity foods.
- Empirical results also show that bloc-member exports often expanded to nonmember markets following the start of the agreement. This finding supports the view that RTA liberalization often spills over into other markets, increasing member exports to nonmember importers. Given that RTAs grant preferential treatment to members, the rise in extra-bloc trade was understandably less than the increase in intra-bloc trade (with the exception being extra-bloc trade involving members of the Association of Southeast Asian Nations Free Trade Agreement, or ASEAN).
- In some markets, nonmember exporters of food bore the cost of RTA formation. Members of ASEAN, the EU, the Common Market for Eastern and Southern Africa (COMESA), the Greater Arab Free Trade Area (GAFTA), and the South Asian Preferential Trade Arrangement (SAPTA) were found to have lowered food imports from extra-bloc exporters following implementation of the

agreements. The adverse effects of four of these RTAs were more pronounced for the United States than for other nonmember exporters. COMESA diverted trade in commodity foods away from non-U.S. exporters, but it did not curtail imports of food from U.S. suppliers.

How Was the Study Conducted?

ERS adopted the gravity framework and estimated benchmark and generalized equations to quantify the effects of 11 specific RTAs on intra- and extra-bloc trade in commodity and manufactured food markets. Data used in the applied analysis include 31 years of bilateral trade flows and selected socioeconomic characteristics of 69 countries and all partner pairs covering the 1975-to-2005 timeframe. To isolate the dimensions of trade creation and trade diversion attributable to each of the RTAs, the benchmark models accounted for such factors underlying trade as bilateral exchange rates, relative factor endowments, transportation costs, and membership/nonmembership in the various RTAs. The generalized models incorporated country-pair effects. By fixing these effects, the generalized equations embody nonobservable factors affecting trade. Both theory and statistical criteria were used to differentiate and identify the preferred analytical approach.

INTRODUCTION

Trade agreements are policy instruments used to reduce cross-border protection and to open markets. The primary goal of the World Trade Organization (WTO) and its predecessor organization, the Generalized Agreement on Tariffs and Trade (GATT), is to contribute to economic development and growth by reducing the obstacles to international trade and helping to ensure a level playing field for all member countries. The GATT/WTO provides a legal and institutional framework for governing cross-border trade between member nations. The “most-favored-nation” (MFN) principle in Article 1 is the centerpiece of the GATT/WTO. According to the MFN provision, each WTO member is to grant all members the same advantage, privilege, favor, or immunity that it grants to any other country. In other words, the provision implies that member countries are not to discriminate in their trade policy against other members.

A challenge facing the WTO and its member countries is reaching consensus about the rules governing international commerce, given the diversity of national sovereignty issues and vested interests. The current stalemate in the Doha Development Agenda (DDA) of the WTO reflects the difficulty of achieving agreement about trade policy reforms at the multilateral level. A former U.S. Trade Representative recently noted that the DDA may be doomed, but reciprocal trade agreements (RTAs) involving bilateral and regional groupings of countries are not (Schwab, 2011). According to Pascal Lamy, the Director-General of the WTO, these preferential agreements "will form part of the long-term tapestry of international trade relations" (World Bank, 2011).

RTAs offer an alternative approach to bargaining for mutual reduction of trade barriers within the framework of the WTO. It is easier for policymakers to reach agreement when there are relatively few countries engaged in negotiations. Still, RTAs may distort markets and divert trade away from efficient nonmember suppliers due to preferential cross-border treatment granted to member countries.

RTAs (i.e., free-trade agreements, customs unions, and common markets) are not consistent with Article I of the MFN provision. They are, however, allowed under Article XXIV. The key requirement of Article XXIV is that the exchange of preferences not be partial (i.e., the removal of duties and other restrictive regulations of commerce are to apply to "substantially all trade" in products between members). The meaning and interpretation of the word "substantial," however, is not clear (Crawford and Laird, 2000; WTO, 2000).

Economists began examining the implications of RTAs for the global trading system during the first wave of countries joining trading blocs in the 1990s. Some observers saw RTAs as "stumbling blocs" to freer trade RTAs, while others saw them as "building blocs." Bhagwati (1991; 1994; 1995), an ardent supporter of the GATT/WTO, repeatedly expresses concern that expansion in the number of RTAs was generating a "spaghetti bowl" of tariffs whereby countries subject the same product to different tariff rates depending on its ostensible origin. Bhagwati believes that RTAs are likely to spawn a complex web of protection across products and countries, reproducing the chaos of the 1930s protectionism. Bhagwati and Panagariya (1996) are skeptical of the ability of RTAs to generate net welfare gains. Both clearly consider adherence to the MFN principle critical to the success of trade policy.

Bergsten (1996, 1998) questions whether the GATT/WTO provides the only, or even the most effective, way to open markets and promote trade liberalization. Bergsten coins the phrase "competitive liberalization" to describe "the overarching force" behind the proliferation of RTAs. According to Bergsten, the increase of global interdependence has induced countries to create RTAs to compete for footloose international investments. He argues that countries belonging to RTAs are better able and more willing to adopt bold trade liberalization reforms than are possible via multilateral trade negotiations within the GATT/WTO. Estevadeordal et al. (2008) show that some RTAs lower tariffs on imports from both member partners and nonmember partners.

Clearly, RTAs have become an increasingly prominent feature in the global marketplace in recent years. Vicard (2009) observes that 14 percent of country pairs trading in 2005 were members of RTAs, up from 4 percent in 1980. But trade flows between RTA partners represented one-third of world trade. This implies that countries belonging to RTAs trade intensively with each other. Crawford and Fiorentino (2005) note that the world has entered into one of the most prolific periods of RTA formations in history. Moreover, the post-1990 wave of RTA formation shows no sign of abating. As of July 2010, the WTO is monitoring 283 agreements, up from 180 agreements in 2003, less than 100 agreements in 1995, and just 40 agreements in 1990.

The rapid expansion of RTAs raises questions. U.S. policymakers have expressed concern, for example, that the large number of RTAs to which the United States does not belong may be eroding U.S. presence in foreign markets. Economists acknowledge that RTAs can provide "stepping stones" toward a more open world market or can, alternatively, be instruments that undermine global free trade and support for multilateral free trade (Krueger, 2000; Andriamananjara, 2003). Quantitative analysis is needed to provide empirical evidence that clarifies the benefits and costs of these agreements.

Econometric studies based on the gravity framework have been used to gauge the impact of RTAs on the volume of trade.[1] A principal objective of the majority of such gravity studies is to estimate intra-bloc trade expansion, often referred to as trade creation, of these agreements.[2] Intra-bloc trade involves trade between members of the same agreement. Perhaps the focus on intra-bloc trade creation stems from policymaker requests for information on the most tangible gains from RTAs.

Panagariya (2000) notes that there is a tendency to ignore possible welfare losses derived from RTAs, especially with respect to nonmember countries. He posits that the concepts of trade creation and trade diversion[3] are central to the policy debates about RTAs and that empirical analysis of these concepts are a challenging, albeit important, area for research. To infer the welfare effects of RTAs, Panagariya advocates applied analysis of trade creation and trade diversion by sector.

"Trade creation" occurs when products from low-cost producers in member countries displace high-cost domestic production. To date, relatively little attention has been given to the impact of RTAs on the reduction of trade between member and nonmember countries, often described as "trade diversion."[4] Trade diversion takes place when bloc countries reorient their trade away from low-cost, nonmember countries toward higher cost, bloc suppliers. Applied research that restricts attention to the intra-bloc impact of RTAs without also examining the extra-bloc trade effects (also known as third-country effects) does not fully examine the role of these agreements in shaping international trade patterns.

A recent ERS study deploys *generic* trade-creation and trade-diversion indexes in gravity equations to identify the impacts on agricultural trade of mutual as well as asymmetric RTA membership (Vollrath and Hallahan, 2011). Mutual RTA membership refers to cases where both the exporter and the importer belong to the same bloc agreement. Asymmetric membership is consigned to cases when the exporter is not a member of an RTA to which the importer belongs. Vollrath and Hallahan find that mutual RTA membership typically expands trade while asymmetric membership reduces partner trade in the world agricultural marketplace. The current study uses gravity models to quantify the intra- and extra-bloc effects of *individual* RTAs on trade in agriculture. Intra-bloc trade refers to cases when trading partners belong to the same agreement. Extra-bloc trade is consigned to cases when either exporting partners or importing partners, but not both, belong to a common RTA. Unlike previously published research, this study controls for source-specific extra-bloc trade diversion. Moreover, it differentiates between the impacts of individual RTAs on U.S. and other competing suppliers who are not members of individual RTAs under consideration. More specifically, this study quantifies the impacts of 11 RTAs on trade in the commodity and manufactured food markets. The 11 agreements examined are the Andean Free Trade Agreement (ANDE), the Association of Southeast Nations Free Trade Agreement (ASEAN), the Central American Common Market (CACM), the Closer Economic Relations (CER), the Common Market for Eastern and Southern Africa (COMESA), the European Union (EU), the Greater Arab Free Trade Area (GAFTA), the Southern Common Market (MERCOSUR), the Canada-U.S. Free Trade Agreement/ North American Free Trade Agreement (NAFTA), the South African Development Community (SADC), and the South Asian Preferential Trade Arrangement (SAPTA).

Collectively, the 11 agreements captured 78 to 92 percent of world agricultural trade during the 1975-2005 period. These agreements are widely distributed throughout the globe. The CER, EU, and NAFTA consist mostly of high-income, industrialized countries. The eight other agreements comprise developing countries. (See table 1 for more detailed information about the set of RTAs selected for this study.)

Table 1. Reciprocal Trade Agreements

Acronym	Agreement name	Initial date	Country membership (1975-2005)*
ANDE	Andean Free Trade Agreement	1996	Bolivia, Colombia, Ecuador, Peru, Venezuela
ASEAN	Association of Southeast Asian Nations Free Trade Agreement	1993	Brunei, Cambodia, Indonesia, Laos, Malaysia, Myanmar, Philippines, Singapore, Venezuela, Thailand
CACM	Central American Common Market	1991	Costa Rica, El Salvador, Guatemala, Honduras, Nicaragua
CER	Closer Economic Relations	1983	Australia, New Zealand
COMESA	Common Market for Eastern & Southern Africa	1995	Angola, Burundi, Comoros, Democratic Republic of the Congo, Djibouti, Egypt, Eritrea, Ethiopia, Kenya, Madagascar, Malawi, Mauritius, Namibia, Rwanda, Seychelles, Sudan, Swaziland, Uganda, Zambia, Zimbabwe
EU	European Union	1975	Austria, Belgium, Czech Republic, Denmark, Finland, France, Malta, Netherlands, Germany, Greece, Hungary, Ireland, Italy, Latvia, Lithuania, Luxembourg, Poland, Portugal, Slovakia, Slovenia, Spain, Sweden, United Kingdom
GAFTA	Greater Arab Free Trade Area	1998	Egypt, Jordan, Kuwait, Morocco, Saudi Arabia, Tunisia
MERC	Mercosur Free Trade Agreement	1995	Argentina, Brazil, Paraguay, Uruguay
NAFTA	North American Free Trade Agreement	1989	Canada, Mexico, United States
SADC	South African Development Community	2001	Angola, Botswana, Lesotho, Malawi, Mauritius, Mozambique, Namibia, South Africa, Swaziland, Zambia, Zimbabwe
SAPTA	South Asian Preferential Trade Arrangement	1996	Bhutan, Bangladesh, India, Pakistan, Moldova, Nepal, Sri Lanka

* Country membership coded dynamically in the regression models as countries entered/exited from the agreements.

Note: Data on the 11 RTAs and their date of entry into force were compiled by scrutinizing previously published gravity studies and multiple websites, including the WTO homepage.

Commodity foods include raw ingredients (e.g., grains, nuts, fruit, and vegetables) as well as semi-processed products (e.g., preserved fruit and vegetables, meats, and dairy products). They are widely traded throughout the world because of the global distribution of relatively fixed land and labor supply (Regmi et al., 2005). Manufactured foods are highly processed products (e.g., breakfast cereal, bakery products, pasta, candy, beer, soft drinks, soups, infant formula, and other food preparations). They are also extensively traded throughout the world even though the location of production of these foods is less dependent on the domestic availability of natural resources.

In today's globalized economy, manufacturing firms produce finished consumer foods in almost every country because raw agricultural inputs, such as grains, flour, and vegetables oils, can be easily sourced. If inputs are not available domestically, they can be readily imported from foreign suppliers—unless raw-material imports are constrained by cross-border trade barriers.

Theoretical and Applied Models

A recent study at the Organisation for Economic Co-operation and Development (OECD) examined a large number of RTAs and found evidence that they had contributed to agricultural trade liberalization (OECD, 2010). The empirical methodology adopted by OECD focused on the share of tariff lines that became zero as a result of RTAs.[5] It did not evaluate other modes of protection (e.g., regulatory mechanisms, technical barriers to trade, sanitary and phytosanitary measures). A methodology that does not quantify nontariff barriers is inherently limited, especially in view of the post-1995 shift toward such barriers following implementation of the Uruguay Round Agreement on Agriculture.

Gravity models provide a means to identify the extent to which RTAs affect trade and trade liberalization that go beyond the narrow focus on tariffs alone. Parameter estimates derived from gravity equations quantify positive/negative deviations in trade that characterize RTAs from hypothesized counterfactual levels in their absence—conditional on the other regressors in the estimating equations. These econometric models are, therefore, capable of isolating the impact of RTAs on trade flows, an issue that the authors of the OECD study explicitly acknowledge as one that merits further research.

In this study, the gravity framework is used in conjunction with panel data spanning trade between 69 countries from 1975 through 2005 to quantify how

11 RTAs have shaped the pattern of world trade in commodity and manufactured foods.[6,7] Benchmark and generalized models are estimated to measure the "treatment effects" of 11 RTAs on intra- and extra-bloc trade in the two food markets.[8]

The Analytical Framework

Gravity models have been widely deployed to gain a better understanding of the forces underlying trade. Tinbergen (1962) was the first to estimate such a model. He posited that the volume of trade between two countries was a function of their "masses" (proxied by Gross Domestic Product or population) and the distance separating them. Linnemann (1966) provided the first economic framework underlying the gravity model of international trade. He showed that the basic model could be derived from a four-equation partial equilibrium model of export supply and import demand.[9] Linnemann was also the first to include RTA membership as an explanatory variable.

Theoretical advances and improvements in model specification of gravity equations have been made since the pioneering work of Tinbergen and Linnemann. (See Anderson, 1979; Helpman and Krugman, 1985; Bergstrand, 1985, 1989, and 1990; Deardorff, 1998; Evenett and Keller, 2002; Anderson and van Wincoop, 2003 and 2004; Feenstra, 2002 and 2004; Baldwin, 2006; and Baier and Bergstrand (2007).)

In this study, all of the applied models are estimated using longitudinal rather than cross-sectional data. The employment of panel data creates greater efficiency, more variability, and less collinearity among the independent variables and is, therefore, generally preferred (Baltagi, 2001). Moreover, the use of panel data is particularly advantageous in estimation of econometric models that incorporate RTA dummy variables. Sohn and Lee (2006) contend that any empirical examination of the impacts of RTAs should incorporate longitudinal data rather than just a single point in time to allow for the phaseout of trade barriers. Baier et al. (2008) observe that "panel data offer an opportunity to better identify unbiased effects" of RTAs on trade flow than cross-section models because implementation of RTAs is typically slow moving, whereas changes in trade flows occur rapidly. Importantly, panel-based models enable the researcher to enrich model specification with fixed effects that potentially mitigate omitted-variable and heterogeneity bias. The statistical framework encompassing conventional gravity models using panel data is characterized as follows:

$$\ln(X_{ijt}) = \alpha_0 + \beta z'_{ijt} + \varepsilon_{ijt} \tag{1}$$

where X_{ijt} denotes trade from country i to country j in year t, z' is the vector of variables representing the export supply and import demand factors affecting partner trade, and ε_{ijt} is the idiosyncratic error assumed to have a distribution characterized by a mean of zero and a constant variance. The independent variables include country-specific characteristics, such as the GDP of each country in year t, and other factors common to both countries that affect bilateral trade, such as symmetric or asymmetric RTA memberships in time t.

Mátyás (1997) points out that model (1) imposes "unnecessary" restriction, namely that $\alpha_i = \alpha_j = \alpha_t = 0$ for all i, j, and t. He contends that the correct econometric specification takes the form of a triple-indexed model, with α_t capturing cyclic influences shared by all countries and α_i and α_j capturing exporter and importer fixed effects, respectively:

$$\ln(X_{ijt}) = \alpha_0 + \alpha_i + \alpha_j + \alpha_t + \beta z'_{ijt} + \varepsilon_{ijt} \tag{2}$$

Mátyás's three fixed-effect approach has been criticized for being a restricted version of a more general model. Egger and Pfaffermayr (2003) note that model (2) does not span the whole vector space explaining variations in bilateral exports. They posit that the proper specification of gravity equations includes exporter-to-importer fixed effects (α_{ij}), in addition to Mátyás's three-way effects:

$$\ln(X_{ijt}) = \alpha_0 + \alpha_i + \alpha_j + \alpha_t + \alpha_{ij} + \beta z'_{ijt} + \varepsilon_{ijt} \tag{3}$$

To circumvent perfect collinearity in the estimation of the above model, one α_i and one α_j must be set to zero. The removal of an exporter-fixed and an importer-fixed effect imposes a series of cross-pair restrictions on α_{ij}*'s*. Due to orthogonality, model (3) is equivalent to the following two-way model with time and country-pair fixed effects:

$$\ln(X_{ijt}) = \alpha_0 + \alpha_i + \alpha_j + \alpha_t + \alpha_{ij} + \beta z'_{ijt} + \varepsilon_{ijt} \tag{3`}$$

The inclusion of α_{ij}. in model (3`) mitigates heterogeneity bias by relaxing the restriction that the intercept of the gravity equation must be the same for all trading pairs. The α_{ij} vector accounts for the many variables commonly specified in gravity equations, such as distance, as well as the many difficultto-quantify and/or unobservable variables that are specific to cross-sectional units over time.

The Benchmark and Generalized Food Models

Our "benchmark gravity model" is designed to capture the impact of specific economic factors commonly believed to drive commodity and manufactured food trade between countries. This model, which is consistent with the traditional gravity framework, contains (1) time-varying covariates (i.e., exporter and importer incomes, relative factor endowments, bilateral exchange-rate misalignments, and indicators of mutual and asymmetric RTA membership) and (2) time-invariant dyadic variables denoting transaction costs (i.e., distance, contiguity, common language, colonial heritage, and indicators of partner countries being landlocked). The basic model is expressed as follows:

$$
\begin{aligned}
\ln(X_{ijt}) &= \alpha_0 + \alpha_t + \beta_1 \ln(Y_{it}) + \beta_2 \ln(Y_{jt}) + \beta_3 \ln(EM_{ijt}) + \beta_4 \ln(FE_{ijt}) \\
&+ \beta_5 \ln(DT_{ij}) + \beta_6(CB_{ij}) + \beta_7(LL_{ij}) + \beta_8(LS_{ij}) + \beta_9(CH_{ij}) + \sum_r \delta_1^r(ITC_{ijt}^r) \\
&+ \sum_r \delta_2^r(XTC_{ijt}^r) + \sum_r \gamma_1^r(MTD_{USjt}^r) + \sum_r \gamma_2^r(MTD_{OTHjt}^r) + \mu_{ijt}
\end{aligned} \qquad (4)
$$

Xijt is the value of trade between exporter *i* and importer *j* in year *t*. GDP quantifies market size, with Y_{it} representing the potential supply of goods from exporter *i* in year *t* and Y_{jt} gauging the potential demand of goods being traded by importer *j* in year *t*. EM_{ijt} is an indicator of bilateral-exchangerate misalignment. It is modeled after Perée and Steinherr's (1989) measure of exchange-rate uncertainty and Rosenberg's (2003) measure of the purchasing-power equilibrium exchange rate.[10,11] Relative factor endowments are captured by FE_{ijt}, a measure of exporter-to-importer arable-land/ total-labor ratios in year *t*. The indicators for transportation costs include physical distance DT_{ij} and two indicator variables to reflect geographical characteristics, CB_{ij}, which equals 1 when *i* and *j* share a contiguous border and 0 otherwise and a landlocked variable LL_{ij}, which equals 1 when either *i* and/or *j* are landlocked and 0 otherwise. The measures for cultural proximity include language similarity LS_{ij}, an indicator variable which equals 1 whenever 9 percent or more of the population in both countries share a common language and 0 otherwise;[12] and colonial heritage $CH_{ij,}$ an indicator variable that equals 1 if two countries have established colonial ties since 1945 and 0 otherwise. Time dummies (α_t) account for factors common to all countries, including worldwide inflation, increases in trade attributable to globalization, and general shocks affecting the world economy,[13] and μ_{ijt} is an idiosyncratic error.

The RTA bivariate variables in equation (4) enable different dimensions of trade creation/diversion to be quantified for each of the 11 RTAs.[14] They include (1) $ITC^r ijt^{r,}$ a dummy variable that equals 1 when i and j are both members of agreement r in year t and 0 when either i or j do not belong to r in year t; (2) $XTC^r{}_{ijt}$, a dummy variable that equals 1 when i is a member of agreement r and j is not a member of agreement r in year t and 0 otherwise; (3) $MTD^r{}_{USjt}$, a dummy variable that equals 1 when the United States, as an exporter, is not a member of agreement r to which j belongs in year t and 0 otherwise; and (4) $MTD^r{}_{OTHjt}$, a dummy variable that equals 1 when the non-U.S. exporter is not a member of agreement r to which j belongs in year t and 0 otherwise.

The variables of particular interest in this study are the intra-bloc ($ITC^r{}_{ijt}$) and three extra-bloc RTA-dummies ($ITC^r{}_{ijt}$ $MTD^r{}_{USjt}$ $MTD^r{}_{OTHjt}$). The hypothesized signs and descriptions of these covariates are as follows:

- $\delta_1{}^r > 0$ denotes intra-bloc trade creation for agreement r.
- $\delta_2{}^r > 0$ denotes extra-bloc trade creation for the set of countries belonging to agreement r exporting to partners not members of bloc r.
- $\gamma_1{}^r < 0$ denotes import trade diversion adversely affecting the United States as a foreign supplier that lowers U.S. exports to trading bloc r.
- $\gamma_2{}^r < 0$ denotes import trade diversion that lowers non-U.S.-foreign suppliers' exports to agreement r.

Clearly, factors other than those specified in the benchmark models are likely to influence both the level of partner trade as well as motivations for countries to enter into mutual RTAs. Examples include nontariff barriers, shipping regulations, antitrust rules, product standards, and other behind-the-border constraints.[15] Despite their potential importance, covariates denoting such factors are often not included in gravity equations as they are either not observable or are nearly impossible to quantify. Should the omitted factors be, in fact, correlated with countries' decisions to forge trading agreements, the generated RTA coefficients capture more than just the effects of these agreements. Hence, parameter estimates obtained from benchmark models may be biased and/or inconsistent due to omitted variable bias.

Another statistical issue of potential concern is endogeneity bias. Baier and Bergstrand (2007) posit that the primary source of such bias in the majority of applied econometric trade models is unobserved heterogeneity. The intuition behind their concern can be illustrated in the case of "natural trading partners." Consider the United States and Canada. Both countries are viewed as being natural trading partners. They share a common culture, speak the same language, have comparable institutional structures, and possess other affinities (e.g., similar values, tastes, and preferences). As a result, the United States and Canada are more likely to reach bilateral or regional trade agreements for reasons other than those captured by the variables specified in conventional gravity equations. Endogeneity bias is, therefore, likely to occur in such equations as the RTA dummy variables that denote joint or asymmetric RTA membership involving the United States and/or Canada and may be correlated with the error term. Hence, the absence of variables denoting affinity factors in estimating equations can lead to omitted-variable bias should they be systematically correlated with both bilateral trade and the RTA covariates.

The second type of gravity model used in this study mitigates both omitted-variable and endogeneity bias. It deploys exporter-to-importer fixed effects in lieu of the time-invariant variables in the benchmark model. Our "generalized gravity model" is expressed as follows:

$$\ln(X_{ijt}) = \alpha_0 + \alpha_t + \alpha_{ij} + \beta_1 \ln(Y_{it}) + \beta_2 \ln(Y_{jt}) + \beta_3 \ln(EM_{ijt}) + \beta_4 \ln(FE_{ijt}) + \sum_r \delta_1^r (ITC_{ijt}^r) + \sum_r \delta_2^r (XTC_{ijt}^r) + \sum_r \gamma_1^r (MTD_{USjt}^r) + \sum_r \gamma_2^r (MTD_{OTHjt}^r) + \varepsilon_{ijt} \tag{5}$$

The exporter-to-importer fixed effects (α_{ij}) generate country-pair intercepts. They isolate the trade creation/diversion impacts of each agreement r from the influence of other dyadic determinants, whether the latter are observable or nonobservable, by virtue of their ability to allow each unidirectional bilateral trade flow to have its own intercept. These country-pair fixed effects embody many difficult, if not impossible, to quantify factors, such as the natural-trading-partner phenomenon characterizing two countries (e.g., the United States and Canada) that induce in some partners trading proportionally more with each other than with others even in the absence of trade agreements (e.g., NAFTA). Hence, equation (5) accounts for heterogeneity more thoroughly than the *ad hoc* set of time-invariant variables (i.e., distance, physical adjacency, common language) in equation (4). Thus, the generalized gravity model enables the trade impacts of the individual RTAs to be separated from the unique bilateral relationships characterizing each country pair. Moreover, the inclusion of the exporter-to-importer fixed effects allays concerns expressed by Bayoumi and Eichengreen (1997) that RTAs serve as "catch basins" for omitted variables in conventional econometric trade models. As Baldwin and Taglioni (2006) put it, the omission of country-pair fixed effects in gravity models, constructed to calibrate the integration effects of RTAs, is a classic example of the "gold medal" error. The country-pair fixed effects account for a range of socio/political/institutional factors that characterize each partner pair. Hence, the inclusion of these effects in estimating equations controls for the correlation between unobservable dyadic effects and the RTA binary variables.

We conclude that the generalized framework, with its exporter-to-importer fixed effects, is conceptually more appropriate than the benchmark framework. We also hypothesize that our generalized gravity equations for commodity and manufactured foods are likely to generate more reliable RTA parameter estimates than the corresponding benchmark equations.

Data

Annual bilateral trade data were obtained from the United Nations (UN) Commodity Trade Statistics (UN Statistical Office, 2007) database, UNComtrade, the primary international trade data source. The ERS panel dataset used in this study was compiled using UN-reported partner trade flows of commodity and manufactured foods among 69 countries from 1975 through 2005. Distances between capital cities and/or the major commercial center closest to partner countries were calculated using the great circle method obtained from USDA's Agricultural Research Service (2005). Data on common borders, language, and landlocked countries were taken from the website at the Centre d'Etudes Prospectives et d'Informations Internationales (2007). Information about arable land was obtained from the Food and Agriculture Organization of the United Nations (2008) FAOSTAT database. Data on reciprocal trade agreements and their date of entry into force were compiled by scrutinizing previously published gravity studies and multiple websites, including the WTO homepage (2011). All other data were obtained from *World Development Indicators* (see World Bank, 2008). Summary statistics for the variables in the panel dataset are shown in the appendix table.

Empirical Model Selection

In this study, the benchmark and generalized gravity equations are estimated for the commodity- and manufactured-food markets using alternative estimators and functional forms. The econometric results along with cluster-robust standard errors are presented in tables 2 and 3.[16]

Population-average (PA) and random-effects (RE) algorithms are deployed to estimate the benchmark equations, and the fixed-effects (FE) algorithm is used to estimate the generalized equations.[17]A statistical advantage of the PA and RE models is that all coefficients, including those for the time-invariant variables, can be estimated. A disadvantage is that their parameter estimates are inconsistent if the fixed-effects (FE) estimator is found to be appropriate. All of our log-linear gravity models are estimated using ordinary-leastsquares (OLS) techniques. A shortcoming of this approach is that OLS omits trade observations that are zero because the log of zero is undefined. Truncation of datasets used in empirical analysis may cause problems by deleting information that leads to bias estimates.[18] To address possible selection bias that may occur when not using the full panel dataset that includes both positive and zero trade flows, we estimate gravity equations using the Poisson-pseudo-maximum-likelihood (PPML) technique proposed by Santos Silva and Tenreyro (2006). Diagnostic statistical tests are used to help identify the most appropriate empirical models to best gauge the RTA impacts on food trade. To evaluate the appropriateness of the RE estimator for our commodity and manufactured food trade models, we followed Egger and deployed the Hausman test, using the method of Wooldridge (2002).[19] The null hypothesis under the Hausman test is that the RE estimator is preferred to the PA alternative. This hypothesis is rejected in all cases at the .01 level of significance using Wald tests (see, column 2 in tables 2 and 3). The Hausman test results are consistent with Egger's empirical findings for total merchandise trade. We conclude that the PA estimator is the preferred approach to estimate the benchmark food equations. The generalized gravity equations are estimated using the OLS and PPML techniques. The conventional practice is to use OLS. A shortcoming of this procedure is that information is lost whenever the trade matrix used does not include zero observations and is, therefore, unbalanced. We used Stata's *areg* procedure, which absorbs the country-pair fixed effects via centering, to estimate the log-linear models and its *xtpqml* procedure to estimate the corresponding Poisson models. The PPML model for commodity foods did not converge.[20] Statistical criteria show that OLS is the most appropriate technique for estimating the generalized equation for processed food. Goodness-of-fit statistics clearly favor the OLS estimator. Witness the considerably larger Aikake information-criterion (AIC) penalty for the Poisson model vis-à-vis the AIC for the OLS model.

As a further check on the adequacy of the OLS in comparison with the PPML estimator, we performed heteroskedasticity-robust, regression-equationspecification-error tests. The null hypothesis for the Ramsey RESET test is clearly rejected for the PPML estimator for processed foods but not for the OLS estimator in either the commodity food or the processed food equations (see column 6 in table 2 and columns 3 and 6 in table 3).[21] These findings suggest that omitted variables are a source of errors-in-variable bias in the PPML estimation, a problem that is not apparent in the OLS equation.

Table 2. Benchmark and generalized models results for commodity foods

	Benchmark models		Generalized models		
	PA model	RE model		FE models	
Variables	LICs &HICs (1)	LICs &HICs (2)	LICs &HICs (3)	LICs (4)	HICs (5)
ln(Yi)	0.58**	0.45**	0.01	0.02	0.01
	(0.02)	(0.02)	(0.04)	(0.04)	(0.04)
ln(Yj)	0.76**	0.84**	0.81**	0.81**	0.80**
	(0.02)	(0.02)	(0.04)	(0.04)	(0.04)
ln(EMijt)	-0.06*	-0.09**	-0.09**	-0.09**	-0.11**
	(0.03)	(0.02)	(0.02)	(0.02)	(0.02)
ln(FEijt)	0.18**	0.16**	0.04	0.06	0.05
	(0.01)	(0.02)	(0.04)	(0.04)	(0.04)
ln(DTij)	-0.83**	-0.95**			
	(0.04)	(0.04)			
CBij	0.47**	0.78**			
	(0.16)	(0.19)			
LLij	-0.36**	-0.55**			
	(0.08)	(0.09)			
LSij	0.48**	0.29**			
	(0.07)	(0.09)			
CHij	1.68**	2.00**			
	(0.19)	(0.23)			
ITC^{ANDE}	3.01**	1.47**	1.40**	1.38**	
	(0.49)	(0.09)	(0.09)	(0.09)	
XTC^{ANDE}	-0.08	0.11	0.08	0.04	
	(0.21)	(0.12)	(0.13)	(0.13)	
MTD^{ANDE_US}	1.76**	-0.33	-0.34	-0.34	
	(0.24)	(0.27)	(0.29)	(0.29)	
$MTD^{ANDE\_non\text{-}US}$	-0.91**	0.01	0.11	0.11	
	(0.18)	(0.12)	(0.13)	(0.13)	
ITC^{ASEAN}	2.17**	0.24	0.21	0.19	

Table 2. (Continued)

Variables	Benchmark models		Generalized models		
	PA model	RE model		FE models	
	LICs &HICs (1)	LICs &HICs (2)	LICs &HICs (3)	LICs (4)	HICs (5)
	(0.25)	(0.24)	(0.24)	(0.24)	
XTC^{ASEAN}	1.99**	0.31**	0.27**	0.23**	
	(0.11)	(0.08)	(0.08)	(0.08)	
MTD^{ANSEAN_US}	1.20*	0.04	-0.02	-0.01	
	(0.49)	(0.26)	(0.24)	(0.24)	
$MTD^{ASEAN\_non\text{-}US}$	0.10	0.01	0.04	0.04	
	(0.12)	(0.09)	(0.10)	(0.10)	
ITC^{CACM}	3.18**	1.09**	0.95**	0.93**	
	(0.22)	(0.25)	(0.29)	(0.29)	
XTC^{CACM}	1.17**	-0.10	-0.17	-0.21*	
	(0.13)	(0.09)	(0.09)	(0.09)	
MTD^{CACM_US}	2.05**	0.28	0.14	0.16	
	(0.21)	(0.16)	(0.16)	(0.16)	
$MTD^{CACM\_non\text{-}US}$	-0.56**	0.43**	0.58**	0.58**	
	(0.12)	(0.08)	(0.09)	(0.09)	
ITC^{CER}	2.90**	1.24**	0.63**		0.58**
	(0.18)	(0.05)	(0.08)		(0.08)
XTC^{CER}	2.38**	0.98**	0.47**		0.43**
	(0.16)	(0.13)	(0.16)		(0.16)
MTD^{CER_US}	0.35*	0.01	-0.42		-0.41
	(0.18)	(0.40)	(0.51)		(0.51)
$MTD^{CER\_non\text{-}US}$	0.56**	0.30**	0.24		0.22
	(0.16)	(0.11)	(0.14)		(0.14)
ITC^{COMESA}	1.98**	1.77**	1.75**	1.74**	
	(0.57)	(0.32)	(0.37)	(0.37)	
XTC^{COMESA}	0.30	0.26**	0.27*	0.23*	
	(0.16)	(0.10)	(0.11)	(0.11)	
MTD^{COMESA_US}	0.96	-0.22	-0.30	-0.29	
	(0.56)	(0.28)	(0.28)	(0.28)	
$MTD^{COMESA\_non\text{-}US}$	-0.25	-0.12	-0.13	-0.13	
	(0.15)	(0.11)	(0.12)	(0.12)	
IT^{CEU}	1.21**	0.86**	0.67**		0.56**
	(0.12)	(0.08)	(0.09)		(0.09)
XT^{CEU}	0.66**	0.20**	0.08		0.02
	(0.07)	(0.06)	(0.07)		(0.07)
MT^{DEU_US}	0.29	-0.63**	-1.08**		-1.10**
	(0.23)	(0.24)	(0.26)		(0.25)
$MT^{DEU\_non\text{-}US}$	0.50**	-0.18**	-0.34**		-0.35**
	(0.09)	(0.06)	(0.07)		(0.07)
ITC^{GAFTA}	0.21	0.51	0.48	0.47	
	(0.36)	(0.27)	(0.29)	(0.29)	
XTC^{GAFTA}	-1.63**	-0.07	0.04	0.00	
	(0.13)	(0.09)	(0.09)	(0.09)	

	Benchmark models		Generalized models		
	PA model	RE model		FE models	
Variables	LICs &HICs (1)	LICs &HICs (2)	LICs &HICs (3)	LICs (4)	HICs (5)
MTD^{GAFTA_US}	0.91*	-0.69**	-0.74**	-0.74**	
	(0.41)	(0.12)	(0.12)	(0.12)	
$MTD^{GAFTA\_non\text{-}US}$	0.35**	-0.34**	-0.36**	-0.36**	
	(0.11)	(0.07)	(0.07)	(0.07)	
ITC^{MERC}	3.43**	0.79**	0.62**	0.61**	
	(0.33)	(0.12)	(0.12)	(0.12)	
XTC^{MERC}	1.90**	0.45**	0.31**	0.27**	
	(0.11)	(0.09)	(0.10)	(0.10)	
MTD^{MERC_US}	-0.06	-0.26	-0.29	-0.28	
	(0.26)	(0.27)	(0.29)	(0.29)	
$MTD^{MERC\_non\text{-}US}$	-0.59**	0.39**	0.46**	0.46**	
	(0.13)	(0.10)	(0.10)	(0.10)	
ITC^{NAFTA}	2.17**	0.63**	0.50**	0.48**	0.40**
	(0.42)	(0.13)	(0.12)	(0.12)	(0.11)
XTC^{NAFTA}	1.21**	0.47**	0.35**	0.30**	0.26**
	(0.12)	(0.08)	(0.09)	(0.09)	(0.09)
$MTD^{NAFTA\_non\text{-}US}$	0.57**	0.15	0.12	0.12	0.09
	(0.13)	(0.08)	(0.09)	(0.09)	(0.09)
ITC^{SADC}	4.16**	0.89**	0.71*	0.71**	
	(1.16)	(0.34)	(0.28)	(0.27)	
XTC^{SADC}	0.75**	0.75**	0.68**	0.65**	
	(0.20)	(0.13)	(0.13)	(0.13)	
MTD^{SADC_US}	0.11	0.16	0.16	0.16	
	(0.37)	(0.53)	(0.57)	(0.57)	
$MTD^{SADC\_non\text{-}US}$	-0.07	0.15	0.18	0.18	
	(0.18)	(0.14)	(0.14)	(0.14)	
ITC^{SAPTA}	2.15**	0.39	0.34	0.32	
	(0.63)	(0.31)	(0.33)	(0.33)	
XTC^{SAPTA}	0.43**	0.31**	0.31**	0.27*	
	(0.15)	(0.10)	(0.11)	(0.11)	
MTD^{SAPTA_US}	1.04**	-1.21**	-1.28**	-1.27**	
	(0.39)	(0.20)	(0.22)	(0.22)	
$MTD^{SAPTA\_non\text{-}US}$	-0.55**	-0.13	-0.10	-0.10	
	(0.15)	(0.09)	(0.10)	(0.10)	
C	15.91**	16.98**	10.85**	10.82**	11.06**
	(0.37)	(0.38)	(0.32)	(0.32)	(0.32)
Observations	89,723	89,723	89,723	89,723	89,723
Number of xm pair		4529			
$\hat{\sigma}_u$		1.84			
$\hat{\sigma}_e$		1.26			
$\hat{\sigma}$		2.23			
ρ		0.681			
$\hat{\Theta}_{50}$		0.864			
R_w^2		0.115			
R_b^2		0.495			
$\chi 2$		10357			

Table 2. (Continued)

Variables	Benchmark models PA model LICs &HICs (1)	RE model LICs &HICs (2)	Generalized models LICs &HICs (3)	FE models LICs (4)	HICs (5)
R^2_{adj}	0.47		0.83	0.83	0.83
AIC	3.99E+05		2.92E+05		
RESET	F = 27.33		F = 1.32		
RESET test p-values	0.0000		0.2512		
F (Hausman)		F = 128.38			
Prob> F		0.0000			

Notes: PA = population-average effects. RE = random effects. FE = fixed effects. LIC = low-income countries. HIC = high-income countries. The dependent variables and all time-varying independent variables are expressed in logarithmic terms. All regressions are estimated using annual panel data from 1975 through 2005. Time- and country-pair-dummy parameter estimates are not reported to save space. Standard errors are in parentheses. They are calculated using White's heteroskedastic robust-standard errors. * and ** denote that the null hypothesis is rejected at the 0.05 and 0.01 level, respectively.

Table 3. Benchmark and generalized models results for manufactured foods

	Benchmark models LICs & HICs		Generalized models	FE (OLS)		FE(PPML)
	PA(OLS)	RE (OLS)	LICs &HICs	LICs	HICs	LICs &HICs
Variables	(1)	(2)	(3)	(4)	(5)	(6)
ln(Yi)	0.83**	0.79**	0.29**	0.29**	0.30**	0.27*
	(0.02)	(0.02)	(0.05)	(0.05)	(0.05)	(0.11)
ln(Yj)	0.61**	0.67**	0.94**	0.95**	0.96**	0.82**
	(0.02)	(0.02)	(0.05)	(0.05)	(0.05)	(0.09)
ln(EMijt)	-0.25**	-0.13**	-0.11**	0.10**	0.11**	-0.07*
	(0.03)	(0.02)	(0.02)	(0.02)	(0.02)	(0.03)
ln(FEijt)	0.04**	0.04*	-0.13*	-0.13*	-0.15**	-0.05
	(0.01)	(0.02)	(0.05)	(0.05)	(0.05)	(0.05)
ln(DTij)	-1.11**	-1.19**				
	(0.04)	(0.04)				
CBij	0.28	0.55**				
	(0.16)	(0.19)				
LLij	-0.11	-0.18*				
	(0.08)	(0.09)				
LSij	0.83**	0.70**				
	(0.07)	(0.08)				
CHij	1.26**	1.54**				
	(0.21)	(0.26)				

	Benchmark models			Generalized models		
	LICs & HICs			FE (OLS)		FE(PPML)
	PA(OLS)	RE (OLS)	LICs &HICs	LICs	HICs	LICs &HICs
Variables	(1)	(2)	(3)	(4)	(5)	(6)
ITC^{ANDE}	2.87**	2.52**	2.45**	2.40**		1.08**
	(0.39)	(0.07)	(0.06)	(0.06)		(0.28)
XTC^{ANDE}	0.46**	0.67**	0.62**	0.60**		0.04
	(0.17)	(0.15)	(0.16)	(0.16)		(0.18)
MTD^{ANDE_US}	0.14	-0.30	-0.23	-0.27		-0.30
	(0.24)	(0.16)	(0.16)	(0.16)		(0.24)
$MTD^{ANDE\_non\text{-}US}$	-0.44*	0.20	0.36*	0.33		0.27
	(0.17)	(0.16)	(0.17)	(0.17)		(0.19)
ITC^{ASEAN}	1.59**	0.90**	0.80*	0.74*		0.05
	(0.32)	(0.33)	(0.34)	(0.34)		(0.22)
XTC^{ASEAN}	1.09**	0.54**	0.50**	0.47**		-0.15
	(0.10)	(0.09)	(0.10)	(0.10)		(0.18)
MTD^{ANSEAN_US}	0.95**	-0.21	-0.36*	-0.39*		-0.19
	(0.36)	(0.17)	(0.17)	(0.17)		(0.14)
$MTD^{ASEAN\_non\text{-}US}$	0.62**	0.36**	0.32**	0.28**		-0.08
	(0.12)	(0.09)	(0.10)	(0.10)		(0.11)
ITC^{CACM}	3.20**	1.11**	0.79*	0.74*		0.55*
	(0.25)	(0.27)	(0.31)	(0.31)		(0.22)
XTC^{CACM}	0.24	-0.18	-0.32	-0.36		-0.60**
	(0.16)	(0.15)	(0.19)	(0.19)		(0.23)
MTD^{CACM_US}	0.67*	-0.03	-0.11	-0.13		0.05
	(0.27)	(0.09)	(0.11)	(0.11)		(0.09)
$MTD^{CACM\_non\text{-}US}$	-0.10	0.24*	0.29*	0.25		0.27
	(0.11)	(0.11)	(0.13)	(0.13)		(0.21)
ITC^{CER}	2.63**	1.96**	1.29**		1.24**	1.66**
	(0.18)	(0.18)	(0.24)		(0.24)	(0.25)
XTC^{CER}	0.67**	0.36**	0.05		-0.02	-0.60
	(0.17)	(0.12)	(0.17)		(0.17)	(0.34)
MTD^{CER_US}	0.26	0.71**	0.50*		0.50*	0.60**
	(0.27)	(0.13)	(0.21)		(0.21)	(0.14)
$MTD^{CER\_non\text{-}US}$	0.83**	0.69**	0.70**		0.70**	0.87**
	(0.14)	(0.13)	(0.16)		(0.16)	(0.16)
ITC^{COMESA}	1.84**	1.56**	1.71**	1.67**		3.30**
	(0.51)	(0.51)	(0.55)	(0.54)		(0.88)
XTC^{COMESA}	-0.01	0.01	0.04	0.02		0.19
	(0.16)	(0.16)	(0.18)	(0.18)		(0.21)
MTD^{COMESA_US}	-0.53	-0.40	-0.36	-0.39		-0.87**
	(0.58)	(0.31)	(0.41)	(0.41)		(0.21)
$MTD^{COMESA\_non\text{-}US}$	-0.71**	-0.41**	-0.42**	-0.44**		-0.56**
	(0.16)	(0.13)	(0.14)	(0.14)		(0.21)
ITC^{EU}	1.41**	0.83**	0.66**		0.56**	0.52**
	(0.13)	(0.09)	(0.10)		(0.10)	(0.09)
XT^{CEU}	1.14**	0.44**	0.18*		0.12	0.06
	(0.08)	(0.06)	(0.07)		(0.08)	(0.07)

Table 3. (Continued)

	Benchmark models			Generalized models		
	LICs & HICs			FE (OLS)		FE(PPML)
	PA(OLS)	RE (OLS)	LICs &HICs	LICs	HICs	LICs &HICs
Variables	(1)	(2)	(3)	(4)	(5)	(6)
MTD^{EU_US}	-0.08	-0.20	-0.28		-0.31	-0.05
	(0.27)	(0.24)	(0.30)		(0.29)	(0.14)
$MTD^{EU\_non\text{-}US}$	-0.25**	0.04	0.15		0.15	0.04
	(0.08)	(0.07)	(0.09)		(0.09)	(0.09)
ITC^{GAFTA}	0.69*	0.39	0.34	0.30		0.38
	(0.32)	(0.23)	(0.25)	(0.25)		(0.25)
XTC^{GAFTA}	-1.56**	-0.19*	-0.03	-0.05		0.17
	(0.13)	(0.10)	(0.10)	(0.10)		(0.24)
MTD^{GAFTA_US}	0.03	-0.66**	-0.67**	0.69**		-0.42**
	(0.61)	(0.15)	(0.15)	(0.15)		(0.08)
$MTD^{GAFTA\_non\text{-}US}$	-0.18	-0.25**	-0.24**	-0.26**		-0.37**
	(0.11)	(0.08)	(0.09)	(0.09)		(0.09)
ITC^{MERC}	2.81**	0.81**	0.67*	0.62		0.27
	(0.40)	(0.30)	(0.33)	(0.33)		(0.20)
XTC^{MERC}	1.00**	0.35**	0.20	0.16		-0.34
	(0.12)	(0.10)	(0.11)	(0.11)		(0.18)
MTD^{MERC_US}	0.81**	0.48	0.50	0.47		0.59**
	(0.24)	(0.27)	(0.27)	(0.26)		(0.18)
$MTD^{MERC\_non\text{-}US}$	-0.41**	0.09	0.22	0.19		-0.08
	(0.13)	(0.11)	(0.11)	(0.11)		(0.20)
ITC^{NAFTA}	1.46**	1.46**	1.37**	1.31**	1.28**	0.72**
	(0.41)	(0.36)	(0.37)	(0.37)	(0.36)	(0.07)
XTC^{NAFTA}	0.29*	0.48**	0.37**	0.34**	0.29**	0.21**
	(0.11)	(0.09)	(0.10)	(0.09)	(0.09)	(0.08)
$MTD^{NAFTA\_non\text{-}US}$	0.47**	0.08	0.04	0.01	0.02	-0.52**
	(0.12)	(0.10)	(0.11)	(0.11)	(0.11)	(0.13)
ITC^{SADC}	2.84*	0.21**	0.03	0.03		0.72**
	(1.30)	(0.05)	(0.14)	(0.14)		(0.16)
XTC^{SADC}	0.25	0.30	0.20	0.18		0.35
	(0.19)	(0.16)	(0.17)	(0.17)		(0.28)
MTD^{SADC_US}	0.00	0.58	0.68	0.66		-0.05
	(0.39)	(0.59)	(0.65)	(0.66)		(0.05)
$MTD^{SADC\_non\text{-}US}$	-0.27	0.13	0.21	0.20		0.26
	(0.20)	(0.16)	(0.17)	(0.17)		(0.21)
ITC^{SAPTA}	-0.05	0.88*	0.94*	0.89*		0.87*
	(0.67)	(0.41)	(0.44)	(0.44)		(0.43)
XTC^{SAPTA}	-0.15	0.29**	0.31**	0.28*		0.01
	(0.14)	(0.11)	(0.12)	(0.12)		(0.14)

	Benchmark models			Generalized models		
	LICs & HICs			FE (OLS)		FE(PPML)
	PA(OLS)	RE (OLS)	LICs &HICs	LICs	HICs	LICs &HICs
Variables	(1)	(2)	(3)	(4)	(5)	(6)
MTD^{SAPTA_US}	-0.42	-1.01**	-1.04**	-1.08**		-1.25**
	(0.36)	(0.23)	(0.27)	(0.27)		(0.05)
$MTD^{SAPTA\_non\text{-}US}$	-0.40**	-0.34**	-0.34**	-0.37**		-0.60**
	(0.13)	(0.10)	(0.10)	(0.10)		(0.12)
C	16.01**	16.07**	7.44**	7.35**	7.19**	
	(0.34)	(0.37)	(0.39)	(0.29)	(0.29)	
Observations	70,954	70,954	70,954	70,954	70,954	102,299
Number of xm pair		4,189				
$\widehat{\sigma_u}$		1.62				
$\hat{\sigma}_e$		1.27				
$\hat{\sigma}$		2.06				
ρ		0.62				
$\hat{\theta}_{50}$		0.83				
R^2_w		0.24				
R^2_b		0.54				
χ^2		17,542				
R^2_{adj}	0.52		0.81	0.81	0.81	
AIC	3.01E+05		2.31E+05			1.96E+11
RESET	F = 15.63		F = 0.48			chi^2 (1)=9.20
RESET test p-values	0.0001		0.4888			0.0024
F (Hausman)		F=187.63				
Prob> F		0.0000				

Notes: PA = population-average effects. RE = random effects. FE = fixed effects. LIC = low-income countries. HIC = high-income countries. All time-varying independent variables are expressed in logarithmic terms. All regressions are estimated using annual panel data from 1975 through 2005. Time- and country-pair-dummy parameter estimates are not reported to save space. Standard errors are in parentheses. They are calculated using White's heteroskedastic robust-standard errors. * and ** denote that the null hypothesis is rejected at the 0.05 and 0.01 level, respectively.

Summary statistics in tables 2 and 3 indicate that the OLS generalized equations are preferred to the benchmark models. Adjusted R^2s show that the generalized gravity models explain more variation than do the corresponding benchmark equations for both the commodity and manufactured food sectors. The overall measures of "goodness of fit" increased from 0.47 to 0.83 [0.52 to 0.81] when comparing the PA-model with the FE-model results for commodity [manufactured] foods (see column 1 and 3 in tables 2 and 3).

Likelihood ratio and Akaike-information-criterion tests do not support the more restricted benchmark models in either food sector, adding further justification favoring the generalized model framework (see columns 1 and 3 in tables 2 and 3). Finally, RESET tests point to omitted-variable bias in the benchmark but not in the generalized equations. This finding addresses Bayoumi and Eichengreen's concern about errors-in-variable bias and Baldwin and Taglioni's intuition of the appropriateness of using country-pair effects when examining the effects of RTAs on trade. Summary measures of overall statistical fit, information-criterion penalties, and both Ramsey RESET and Hausman tests provide support for the generalized gravity models vis-à-vis the benchmark models for both commodity and processed foods. Given our primary interest in this study to quantify the trade impacts of RTAs[22] as well as theoretical considerations and the results of the aforementioned diagnostic tests, we limit discussion in the next section to the RTA parameter estimates using the preferred analytical framework.

Trade Impacts of RTAs

The intra-bloc trade creation (ITC) parameters in table 4 from our preferred generalized gravity equations show that since the time of their inception, 10 of the 11 RTAs expanded trade in either the commodity and/or the manufactured food markets of member countries. The three RTAs that comprise mostly developed countries (i.e., the EU, NAFTA, and CER) increased member-country trade in both the commodity and manufactured food sectors. The formation of the EU increased intra-EU trade in the two food sectors during 1975-2005 between 93 and 95 percent, on average.[23] This translates into a fixed annual increase in food trade between EU countries of 3 percent (table 5).[24] The rise in intra-bloc trade within NAFTA and the CER was, in contrast to that within the EU, substantially greater for manufactured foods than for commodity foods. NAFTA caused trade between member countries to expand 8 percent per year on average in manufactured foods and 3 percent per year in commodity foods between 1989 and 2005. Results for the CER were similar in that the 6-percent annual increase of trade between Australia and New Zealand in manufactured foods was considerably greater than the 3-percent expansion of intra-CER trade in commodity foods.

Table 4. Trade creation and trade diversion parameter estimates for intra- and extra-RTA blocs from the preferred gravity model

		Commodity foods				Manufactured foods		
Agreement	ITC (1)	XTC (2)	MTD^{US} (3)	$MTD^{non\text{-}US}$ (4)	ITC (5)	XTC (6)	MTD^{US} (7)	$MTD^{non\text{-}US}$ (8)
ANDE	1.40**	0.08	-0.34	0.11	2.45**	0.62**	-0.23	0.36*
	(0.09)	(0.13)	(0.29)	(0.13)	(0.06)	(0.16)	(0.16)	(0.17)
ASEAN	0.21	0.27**	-0.02	0.04	0.80*	0.50**	-0.36*	0.32**
	(0.24)	(0.08)	(0.24)	(0.10)	(0.34)	(0.10)	(0.17)	(0.10)
CACM	0.95**	-0.17	0.14	0.58**	0.79*	-0.32	-0.11	0.29*
	(0.29)	(0.09)	(0.16)	(0.09)	(0.31)	(0.19)	(0.11)	(0.13)
CER	0.63**	0.47**	-0.42	0.24	1.29**	0.05	0.50*	0.70**
	(0.08)	(0.16)	(0.51)	(0.14)	(0.24)	(0.17)	(0.21)	(0.16)
COMESA	1.75**	0.27*	-0.30	-0.13	1.71**	0.04	-0.36	-0.42**
	(0.37)	(0.11)	(0.28)	(0.12)	(0.55)	(0.18)	(0.41)	(0.14)
EU	0.67**	0.08	-1.08**	-0.34**	0.66**	0.18*	-0.28	0.15
	(0.09)	(0.07)	(0.26)	(0.07)	(0.10)	(0.07)	(0.30)	(0.09)
GAFTA	0.48	0.04	-0.74**	-0.36**	0.34	-0.03	-0.67**	-0.24**
	(0.29)	(0.09)	(0.12)	(0.07)	(0.25)	(0.10)	(0.15)	(0.09)
MERCOSUR	0.62**	0.31**	-0.29	0.46**	0.67*	0.20	0.50	0.22
	(0.12)	(0.10)	(0.29)	(0.10)	(0.33)	(0.11)	(0.27)	(0.11)
NAFTA	0.50**	0.35**		0.12	1.37**	0.37**		0.04
	(0.12)	(0.09)		(0.09)	(0.37)	(0.10)		(0.11)
SADC	0.71*	0.68**	0.16	0.18	0.03	0.20	0.68	0.21
	(0.28)	(0.13)	(0.57)	(0.14)	(0.14)	(0.17)	(0.65)	(0.17)
SAPTA	0.34	0.31**	-1.28**	-0.10	0.94*	0.31**	-1.04**	-0.34**
	(0.33)	(0.11)	(0.22)	(0.10)	(0.44)	(0.12)	(0.27)	(0.10)

Note: ITC (intra-bloc trade creation), XTC (extra-bloc trade creation), and MTD (import trade diversion) are variables. RTA-parameter estimates and robust standard errors replicated from the ordinary least squares generalized model for commodity (manufactured) foods in tables 2 and 3.

Table 5. RTA-induced average annual percentage change in trade induced by each agreement since inception

		Commodity foods				Manufactured foods		
	Trade creation		Trade diversion		Trade creation		Trade diversion	
Agreement	Intra-bloc (ITC)	Extra-bloc (XTC)	U.S. (MTD^{US})	Non U.S. ($MTD^{non\text{-}US}$)	Intra-bloc (ITC)	Extra-bloc (XTC)	U.S. (MTD^{US})	Non-U.S. ($MTD^{non\text{-}US}$)
ANDE	0.15				0.28	0.06		0.04
ASEAN		0.02			0.06	0.04	-0.03	0.02
CACM	0.07			0.04	0.05			0.02
CER	0.03	0.02			0.06		0.02	0.03

Table 5. (Continued)

		Commodity foods				Manufactured foods		
	Trade creation		Trade diversion		Trade creation		Trade diversion	
Agreement	Intra-bloc (ITC)	Extra-bloc (XTC)	U.S. (MTD^{US})	Non-U.S. ($MTD^{non\text{-}US}$)	Intra-bloc (ITC)	Extra-bloc (XTC)	U.S. (MTD^{US})	Non-U.S. ($MTD^{non\text{-}US}$)
COMESA	0.19	0.03			0.19			-0.04
EU	0.03		-0.03	-0.01	0.03	0.01		
GAFTA			-0.09	-0.04			-0.08	-0.03
MERCOCUR	0.04	0.02		0.03	0.05			
NAFTA	0.03	0.02			0.08	0.02		
SADC	0.15	0.15						
SAPTA		0.03	-0.12		0.10	0.03	-0.10	-0.03

Note:ITC (intra-bloc trade creation), XTC (extra-bloc trade creation), and MTD (import trade diversion) are variables. Percentage average annual change derived from parameter estimates in table 4 that are statistically significant at either the 0.01 or the 0.05 level of significance using the $\left(e^{\delta\frac{1}{n}}-1\right)$ formula where n = the number of years the RTA is in force.

ANDE, CACM, COMESA, and MERC expanded trade with member countries in both food sectors. By contrast, GAFTA had no effect on internal bloc trade in either sector. However, SADC increased intra-bloc trade in commodity foods, and ASEAN and SAPTA augmented trade internally in the manufactured food sector. The finding that some RTAs have not increased cross-border trade with member countries in one or both food markets is not altogether surprising. Many countries, especially those in the developing world, grant limited tariff preferences in agriculture. The lack of statistical significance in commodity-based trade in ASEAN, GAFTA, and SAPTA could reflect the relatively small land bases from which to produce land-intensive commodities. The absence of empirical support for RTA-induced intra-bloc trade-creation could also indicate that food markets are not always well integrated within trading blocs.

Interestingly, model results reveal that not only did most of the RTAs create trade among member countries, but they also expanded trade externally to nonmember countries. Note the positive and statistically significant extra-bloc trade creation (XTCs) coefficients for the agreements that also augmented intra-bloc trade. These results may support Baldwin's (2002) hypothesis that trade liberalization, whether it originates from regional or multilateral agreements, "begets more liberalization." The results may reflect nondiscriminatory reduction in trade barriers to nonmember partners that took place as some of the RTA blocs were lowering barriers to member countries. They may also stem from increases in bloc-country competitiveness arising from spillover efficiencies caused by RTAs that enabled members to increase export sales to nonpartner importers.

Not surprisingly, the RTA-induced trade expansions with external partners were considerably smaller than sales to partner importers when the agreements also augmented intra-bloc trade, except for trade in manufactured foods by ASEAN exporters. The ASEAN countries have little incentive to trade with each other in commodity and manufactured foods given similarities in their members' comparative advantages.

Overall trade creation induced by RTAs, denoted by positive and significant ITC and/or XTC coefficients, depicts most but not all of the agreements in the commodity and manufactured food sectors. Exceptions include nonsignificant parameter estimates for SADC in manufactured foods and for GAFTA in both the commodity and manufactured food sectors. The absence of any statistical significance of trade creation suggests that the set of GAFTA countries is not internationally competitive in either food sector and that the group of SADC countries is not competitive in manufactured foods.

The import-trade-diversion parameter estimates (MTD^{US} and $MTD^{non\text{-}US}$) reveal that 6 of 11 RTAs (i.e., ANDE, CACM, CER, MERCOSUR, NAFTA, and SADC) did not discriminate against outside suppliers.[25] However, both U.S. exporters and the composite foreign supplier in commodity and/ or manufactured food markets were adversely affected by the formation of the EU, GAFTA, and SAPTA. The empirical results show, for example, that the EU reoriented imports of commodity foods away from both outside suppliers. The EU agreement effected a 66-percent decline in U.S. commodity food exports to EU members between 1975 and 2005. This drop is equivalent to an average annual proportional decline in U.S. exports to the EU of 3 percent. The EU had less of an impact on non-U.S. foreign suppliers of commodity foods, with exports falling 29 percent over the entire period, or 1 percent annually, on average. There is no statistical evidence that the EU discriminated against outsider suppliers of manufactured foods.

Results show that countries belonging to GAFTA reoriented imports from the United States and other foreign suppliers in both the commodity and manufactured food sectors. Parameter estimates show that the GAFTA countries lowered food imports from the United States by 8 to 9 percent per year, on average, since GAFTA's inception in 1998. In contrast, GAFTA curtailed imports from non-U.S. suppliers of commodity foods and manufactured foods at average annual rates of 4 percent and 3 percent, respectively.

SAPTA exhibited discriminatory patterns against both U.S. exporters and non-U.S. exporters of manufactured foods. In the manufactured food sector, SAPTA's imports from the United States fell by an annual average of 10 percent from 1996 to 2005, while its imports from the other foreign suppliers declined by 3 percent. In the commodity food sector, SAPTA curtailed its imports from the United States by 12 percent per year, on average. It did not, however, discriminate against non-U.S. foreign suppliers in this sector.

The ASEAN bloc also discriminated against the United States. On average, the ASEAN countries purchased 3 percent less manufactured food from the United States per year during 1993-2005 than would have been the case in the absence of this agreement. In sharp contrast to U.S. exporters, non-U.S. suppliers of manufactured foods to ASEAN actually increased their exports of manufactured foods to countries belonging to this bloc. This pattern suggests that ASEAN is a relatively open agreement overall, but not with respect to U.S. manufactured foods.

The United States also lost export market share to competitors due to the formation of CACM and MERCOSUR. While these two RTA blocs did not directly affect the volume of food imports from the United States, they adversely affected U.S. competitiveness vis-à-vis other suppliers.[26] In each case, bloc-member exporters and non-U.S. foreign suppliers increased sales of commodity and/or manufactured foods in the international marketplace.

COMESA is the only agreement that diverted trade away from non-U.S.-foreign suppliers but not against U.S. exporters. Since its inception in 1995, COMESA curtailed imports of manufactured foods from non-U.S. exporters by 3.5 percent annually. In contrast, imports from the United States did not drop below levels expected in the absence of this agreement.

U.S. food exports to the 10 foreign trading blocs did not increase as a result of RTA formation, except in the case of manufactured food exports to CER, which rose 2 percent per year on average. However, the 6-percent annual increase in trade between Australia and New Zealand and the 3-percent annual increase in non-U.S. suppliers' exports to CER exceeded the rise in U.S. exports of manufactured foods to the CER.

To examine the robustness of model specifications, ERS derived estimates using different combinations of RTAs (see columns 4 and 5 in tables 2 and 3). RTA parameter estimates using the OLS generalized gravity model for both bulk and manufactured foods are virtually identical when comparing food equations containing all 11 RTAs with corresponding regression models that included (1) the subset of RTAs comprising low-income members (i.e., ANDE, ASEAN, CACM, COMESA, GAFTA, MERCOSUR, SADC, and SAPTA) and (2) the subset of high-income RTAs (i.e., CER, EU, and NAFTA). Moreover, the statistical significance of 83 of the 86 parameter comparisons is the same.[27] The empirical results underscore model robustness to different combinations of RTAs.

To obtain information about how RTAs affect trade through time, comparisons are made of model estimations covering a 21-year period (1975-to1994) with those spanning a 31-year period (1975-2005).[28] Not surprisingly, the intra-bloc trade creation coefficients for CACM, ASEAN, and NAFTA (i.e., ITC^{CACM}, ITC^{ASEAN}, and ITC^{NAFTA}) are not significantly different from zero for the 1975-94 period for either food sector. These three agreements entered into force near the end of the early period, in 1991, 1993, and 1994, respectively. Insufficient time elapsed for them to have had a discernable impact on food trade during the 1974-94 period.

As another example of estimated impacts over time, the intra-bloc trade-creation parameter estimates for the CER are positive and significantly different from zero for both the 21- and 31-year time spans. When the two-period ITC coefficients for commodity and manufactured foods (which, understandably, are smaller in magnitude for the shorter time frame) are converted into annual average percentage changes, they reveal that the CER induced greater change in intra-bloc trade creation in the early period—4 percent for commodity foods and 8 percent for manufactured foods—than for the 31-year period as a whole—3 and 6 percent for commodity and manufactured foods, respectively. These results are consistent with findings elsewhere in the literature that show that the impacts of RTA on trade are typically more pronounced during the first 10 to 15 years than afterward (Baier and Bergstrand, 2007; Grant and Lambert, 2008).

To examine more closely the diminishing effect of RTAs on trade through time, generalized gravity models are run covering the first 10 years of four agreements—ASEAN, CACM, CER, and NAFTA—and the 9-year period separating the EU12 from its expansion to the EU15 (following the accession of Austria, Finland, and Sweden). Results are compared with ITC parameter estimates taken from the 1975-2005 model runs. Table 6 shows RTA-induced effects on intra-bloc trade over two timespans for each of the aforementioned RTAs by converting ITC parameter estimates into average annual percentage changes.

In all cases, the empirical results depict larger impacts during the first decade than over the "life" of these agreements. For example, the average annual change of intra-NAFTA trade during the first 10 years of the agreement is 4 percent for commodity foods and 12 percent for manufactured foods. Corresponding figures for the 1975-2005 period as a whole are 3 percent for commodity foods and 8 percent for manufactured foods. In the case of the EU, the average annual percentage change of intra-EU trade through the EU12 period is 7 percent for commodity foods and 6 percent for manufactured foods. The corresponding EU figure for the 1975-2005 period is 3 percent for both commodity foods and manufactured foods.

Table 6. RTA-induced effects on intra-bloc trade over two time periods

Agreement	Commodity foods		Manufactured foods	
	First decade	Through 2005	First decade	Through 2005
ASEAN			0.08	0.06
CACM	0.08	0.07	0.07	0.05
CER	0.04	0.03	0.09	0.06
EU	0.07	0.03	0.06	0.03
NAFTA	0.04	0.03	0.12	0.08

Note: Percentage average annual change derived from parameter estimates that are statistically significant at either the 0.05 or 0.01 level using the formula $\left(e^{\delta\frac{1}{n}}-1\right)$, where n = the number of years the RTA is in force.

SUMMARY AND POLICY IMPLICATIONS

A primary motivation for countries to participate in trade agreements is to increase exports by reducing impediments to trade. Given that the international policy dynamics make negotiating a multilateral trade agreement extremely difficult, countries have resorted to the use of preferential agreements as a practical and feasible route to gain greater access to foreign markets. There are, however, tradeoffs in selecting this policy option. RTAs may become "stepping stones" that lead to more open world markets or "stumbling blocs" that discriminate against efficient suppliers and undermine support for multilateral trade liberalization. Empirical analysis can clarify these effects by gauging the actual impacts of individual agreements.

In this study, gravity models are estimated to identify the effects of 11 RTAs on intra- and extra-bloc trade in commodity and manufactured food markets. Empirical evidence reveals that most RTAs increased food trade in the international marketplace, but some also diverted trade away from more efficient suppliers. Not surprisingly, the rise in exports to partner markets was particularly pronounced when importers belonged to the same RTA as the exporter. The empirical findings also show that bloc-member exports often expanded to nonmember markets. Given the preferential treatment characteristic of RTAs, the rise in this extra-bloc trade was understandably less than the increase in intra-bloc trade, with ASEAN being the notable exception.

Empirical results show that since the time of its inception, the EU curtailed imports of commodity foods from the United States and from non-U.S. suppliers by an annual average of 4 percent and 1 percent, respectively. Such declines accumulate over time. For the 1975-2005 period overall, U.S. commodity food exports to the EU fell 66 percent while exports by non-U.S. suppliers declined 29 percent.[29]

The study also found that U.S. food exporters were more adversely affected than non-U.S. foreign suppliers by three other agreements; namely—ASEAN, GAFTA, and SAPTA. COMESA is the only agreement that diverted food trade from non-U.S. outside suppliers but not from U.S. exporters.

The majority of the 11 trade agreements examined in this study created trade in the commodity and manufactured markets while diverting comparatively little trade away from outside suppliers, with the exception of commodity food imports by the EU. This finding suggests that the benefits of RTAs generally outweigh costs in the international food marketplace. This inference is similar to the conclusion drawn by Vollrath and Hallahan (2011), a study of agricultural trade using generic RTA indexes.

References

Aitken, Norman D. 1973. "The Effect of the EEC and EFTA on European Trade: A Temporal Cross-Section Analysis." *American Economic Review,* Vol. 63: 881-891.

Anderson, James E. 1979. "A Theoretical Foundation for the Gravity Equation." *American Economic Review,* Vol. 69: 106-116, March.

Anderson, James E., and Eric van Wincoop. 2004. "Trade Costs." *Journal of Economic Literature,* Vol. XLII: 691-751, September.

_____. 2003. "Gravity with Gravitas: A Solution to the Border Puzzle." *American Economic Review,* Vol. 93: 170-192, March.

Andriamananjara, Soamiely. 2003. "Competitive Liberalization or Competitive Diversion? Preferential Trade Agreements and the Multilateral Trading System." *Economics Working Paper.* U.S.

International Trade Commission, May. http://papers.ssrn.com/sol3/papers.cfm?abstract_id=405080.

Baier, Scott L, Jeffrey H. Bergstrand, Peter Egger, and Patrick A. McLaughlin. 2008. "Do Economic Integration Agreements Actually Work? Issues in Understanding the Causes and Consequences of Growth of Regionalism." *The World Economy,* Vol. 31: 461-497.

Baier, Scott L., and Jeffrey H. Bergstrand. 2007. "Do Free Trade Agreements Actually Increase Members' International Trade?" *Journal of International Economics,* Vol. 71: 72-95.

Baldwin, Richard. 2002. "Asian Regionalism: Promises and Pitfalls." Seoul, South Korea: KEIP Seminar on East Asia Free Trade Agreements, September 27.

Baldwin, Richard, and Daria Taglioni. 2006."Gravity for Dummies and Dummies for Gravity Equations." NBER Working Paper No. 12516. www.nber.org/papers/w12516.

Baltagi, Badi H. 2001. *Econometric Analysis of Panel Data.* New York: John Wiley & Sons, Ltd.

Bayoumi, Tamim, and Barry Eichengreen. 1997. "Is Regionalism Simply a Diversion? Evidence from the Evolution of the EC and EFTA." In Takatoshi, Ito, and Anne O. Krueger (eds.), *Regionalism Versus Multilateral Trade Arrangements*, pp. 141-164. Chicago: The University of Chicago Press.

Bergsten, C. Fred. 1998. "Fifty Years of the GATT/WTO: Lessons from the Past for Strategies for the Future." Geneva: Fifty Years: Looking Back, Looking Forward. Symposium Paper.

____. 1996. "Competitive Liberalization and Global Free Trade: A Vision for the Early 21st Century." *Working Paper,* 96-15. Institute for International Economics.

Bergstrand, Jeffrey H. 1990. "The Heckscher-Ohlin-Samuelson Model, the Linder Hypothesis, and the Determinants of Bilateral Intra-Industry Trade." *Economic Journal,* Vol. 100: 1216-1229, December.

____. 1989. "The Generalized Gravity Equation, Monopolistic Competition, and the Factor-Proportions Theory in International Trade." *The Review of Economics and Statistics,* Vol. 71: 143-153, February.

____. 1985. "The Gravity Equation in International Trade: Some Microeconomic Foundations and Empirical Evidence." *The Review of Economics and Statistics,* Vol. 67: 474-481, August.

Bhagwati, Jagdish, and Arvind Panagariya. 1996. "Preferential Trading Areas and Multilateralism: Strangers, Friends, or Foes?" In J. Bhagwati and A.

Panagariya (eds.), *The Economics of Preferential Trade Agreements*. Washington, DC.: The American Enterprise Institute Press.

____. 1995. "U.S. Trade Policy: The Infatuation With Free Trade Areas." In J. Bhagwati and A. O. Krueger (eds.), *The Dangerous Drift to Preferential Trade Agreements*. Washington DC.: American Enterprise Institute for Public Policy Research.

____. 1994. "Regionalism and Multilateralism: An Overview.: In Jaime de Melo and Arvind Panagariya (eds.), *New Dimensions in Regional Integration*. Cambridge, UK: Cambridge University Press.

Bhagwati, Jagdish. 1991. *The World Trading System at Risk*. Princeton, NJ: Princeton University Press.

Centre d'Etudes Prospectives et d'Informations Internationales, 2007. Database: *CEPII,* www.cepii.org/anglaisgraph/bdd/distances.htm.

Cernat, Lucian. 2001. "Assessing Regional Trade Arrangements: Are South-South RTAs More Trade Diverting?"*Policy Issues in International Trade and Commodities Study Series,* No. 16. Geneva, Switzerland: United Nations.

Cheng, I-Hui, and Howard J. Wall. 2005. "Controlling for Heterogeneity in Gravity Models of Trade and Integration." *Federal Reserve Bank of St. Louis Review*, Vol. 87(1): 49-63, January/February.

Cho, Guedae, Ian M. Sheldon, and Steve McCorriston. 2002. "Exchange Rate Uncertainty and Agricultural Trade." *American Journal of Agricultural Economics*, Vol. 84: 931-942, November.

Clarete, Ramon, Christopher Edmonds, and Jessica Seddon Wallack. 2003. "Asian Regionalism and Its Effects on Trade in the 1980s and 1990s." *Journal of Asian Economics,* Vol. 14: 91-129.

Crawford, J., and S. Laird. 2000. "Regional Trade Agreements and the WTO." CREDIT Research Paper No. 00/3, Nottingham, UK: CREDIT School of Economics, University of Nottingham, March.

Crawford, Jo-Ann, and Roberto V. Fiorentino. 2005. "The Changing Landscape of Regional Trade Agreements." Discussion Paper No. 8. Geneva, Switzerland: World Trade Organization.

Deardorff, Alan V. 1998. "Determinants of Bilateral Trade: Does Gravity Work in a Neoclassical World?" In J.A. Frankel (ed.), *The Regionalization of the World Economy,* pp. 7-22. Chicago: University of Chicago Press.

Egger, Peter, and Michael Pfaffermayr. 2003. "The Proper Panel Econometric Specification of the Gravity Equation: A Three-Way Model With Bilateral Interaction Effects. *Empirical Economics,* Vol. 28: 571-580.

Egger, Peter. 2000. "A Note on the Proper Econometric Specification of the Gravity Equation." *Economic Letters,* Vol. 66: 25-31.

Eicher, Theo S., and Christian Henn. 2009. "In Search of WTO Trade Effects: Preferential Trade Agreements Promote Trade Strongly, But Unevenly." *IMF Working Paper,* WP/09/31, February. http://econpapers.repec.org/paper/imfimfwpa/09_2f31.htm.

Endoh M. 1999. "Trade Creation and Trade Diversion in the EEC, the LAFTA and the CMEA: 1960-1994." *Applied Economics,* Vol. 31: 207-216.

Estevadeordal, A., C. Freund, and E. Ornelas. 2008. "Does Regionalism Affect Trade Liberalization Towards Non-Members?" *Quarterly Journal of Economics*, Vol. 123(4): 1531-75.

Evenett, Simon J., and Wolfgang Keller. 2002."On Theories Explaining the Success of the Gravity Equation." *Journal of Political Economy,* Vol. 110: 281-316.

Feenstra, Robert C. 2004. *Advanced International Trade: Theory and Evidence.* Princeton, NJ: Princeton University Press.

____. 2002. "Border Effects and the Gravity Equation: Consistent Methods of Estimation." *Scottish Journal of Political Economy*, Vol. 49: 491-506, November.

Food and Agriculture Organization of the United Nations. 2008. FAOSTAT. (available at: faostat.fao.org/faostat/collections?subset=agriculture

Frankel, Jeffrey A. 1997. *Regional Trading Blocs of the World Economic System*. Washington, DC: Institute for International Economics, October.

Frankel, Jeffrey A., and Shang-Jin Wei. 1997. "Regionalization of World Trade and Currencies: Economics and Politics." In Jeffrey Frankel (ed.), *Regional Trading Blocs of the World Economic System*, pp. 189-226. Washington, DC: Institute for International Economics, October.

Grant, Jason H., and Dayton M. Lambert. 2008. "Do Regional Trade Agreements Increase Members' Agricultural Trade?" *American Journal of Agricultural Economics,* Vol. 90: 765-782, August.

____. 2005. "Regionalism in World Agricultural Trade: Lessons from Gravity Model Estimation." Selected Paper, American Agricultural Economics Association Annual Meeting, Providence, RI, July 24-27.

Heckman, James J. 2001. "Policy-Relevant Treatment Effects." *The American Economic Review,* Vol. 91(2): 107-111, May.

Helpman, Elhanan, and Paul R. Krugman. 1985. *Market Structure and Foreign Trade: Increasing Returns, Imperfect Competition, and the International Economy.* Cambridge, MA: MIT Press.

Jayasinghe, Sampath, and Rakhal Sarker. 2008. "Effects of Regional Trade Agreements on Trade in Agrifood Products: Evidence from Gravity Modeling Using Disaggregated Data." *Review of Agricultural Economics,* Vol. 30: 61-81.

Koo, Won W., P. Lynn Kennedy, and Anatoliy Skripnitchenko. 2006. "Regional Preferential Trade Agreements: Trade Creation and Diversion Effects. *Review of Agricultural Economics,* Vol. 28(3): 408-415.

Krueger, Anne O. 2000. "Trade Creation and Trade Diversion Under NAFTA." NBER Working Paper No. 7429, National Bureau of Economic Research.

Lambert, David, and Shahera McKoy. 2009. "Trade Creation and Diversion Effects of Preferential Trade Associations on Agricultural and Food Trade." *Journal of Agricultural Economics*, Vol. 60(1): 17-39.

Lawrence, Robert Z. 1996. *Regionalism, Multilateralism, and Deeper Integration.* The Brookings Institution: Washington, DC, 1996.

Linnemann, Hans. 1966. *An Econometric Study of International Trade Flows.* Amsterdam: North Holland Publishing Co.

Magee, Christopher S.P. 2008. "New Measures of Trade Creation and Trade Diversion."*Journal of International Economics,* Vol. 75: 349-362.

Mátyás, László. 1997. "Proper Econometric Specification of the Gravity Model." *The World Economy,* Vol. 20: 432-434.

Organisation for Economic Development and Co-operation (OECD). 2010. "Treatment of Agriculture in Selected Regional Trade Agreements." Joint Working Party on Agriculture and Trade, November 18th draft.

Panagariya, Arvind. 2000. "Preferential Trade Liberalization: The Traditional Theory and New Developments." *Journal of Economic Literature*, Vol. 38: 287-331, June.

Perée, Eric, and Alfred Steinherr. 1989. "Exchange Rate Uncertainty and Foreign Trade." *European Economic Review,* Vol. 33: 1241-1264.

Regmi, Anita, Mark Gehlhar, John Wainio, Thomas Vollrath, Paul Johnston, and Nitin Kathuria. 2005. *Market Access for High-Value Foods.* Agricultural Economic Report No. 840. U.S. Department of Agriculture, Economic Research Service, February, www.ers.usda.gov/publications/aer840/

Rose, Andrew K., and Eric van Wincoop. 2001. "National Money as a Barrier to International Trade: The Real Case for Currency Union." *The American Economic Review,* Vol. 91: 386-390, May.

Rosenberg, Michael. 2003. "Dollar's Equilibrium Exchange Rate." In C. Fred Bergsten and John Williamson (eds.). *Dollar Overvaluation and the*

World Economy, pp. 36-56. Washington, DC: Institute for International Economics, February.

Sandberg, H. Mikael, James L. Seale, Jr., and Timothy G. Taylor. 2006. "History, Regionalism, and CARICOM Trade: A Gravity Model Analysis." *Journal of Development Studies,* Vol. 42(5): 795-811, July.

Santos Silva, J.M.C., and Silvana Tenreyro. 2006. "The Log of Gravity." *The Review of Economics and Statistics,* Vol. 88: 641-658, November.

Sapir A. 2001. "Domino Effects in Western European Regional Trade, 1960-1992." *European Journal of Political Economy,"* Vol. 17: 377-388.

Sarker, R., and S. Jayasinghe. 2007. "Regional Trade Agreements and Trade in Agri-Food Products: Evidence for the European Union From Gravity Modeling Using Disaggregated Data." *Agricultural Economics,* Vol. 37: 93-104.

Schwab, Susan. 2011. "After Doha: Why the Negotiations Are Doomed and What We Should Do About It." *Foreign Affairs*, Vol. 90(3): 104-118.

Sohn, Chan-Hyun, and Hongshik Lee. 2006. "How FTAs Affect Income Levels of Member Countries. *The World Economy,* Vol. 29: 1737-1757, December.

Sun, Lin, and Michael R. Reed. 2011. "Impacts of Free Trade Agreements on Agricultural Trade Creation and Trade Diversion. *American Journal of Applied Economics,* Vol. 92(5): 1351-1363, January.

Subramanian, Arvind, and Shang-Jin Wei. 2007. "The WTO Promotes Trade, Strongly but Unevenly." *Journal of International Economics,* Vol. 72: 151-175, May.

Tang, Donny. 2005. "Effects of the Regional Trading Arrangements on Trade: Evidence From the NAFTA, ANZCER, and ASEAN Countries, 1989-2000." *Journal of International Trade and Economic Development,* Vol. 14(2): 241-265.

Tinbergen, J. 1962. *Shaping the World Economy.* New York: Twentieth Century Fund.

United Nations Statistical Office. 2007. Database: UN Comtrade. (available at: unstats.un.org/unsd/comtrade/mr/rfReportersList.aspx).

U.S. Department of Agriculture, Agricultural Research Service. 2005. "Surface Distance Between Two Points of Latitude and Longitude." (available at: www.wcrl.ars.usda.gov/cec/java/lat-long.htm).

Vicard, Vincent. 2009. "On Trade Creation and Regional Trade Agreements: Does Depth Matter?" *Review of World Economics,* Vol. 145(2): 167-187, July.

Viner, Jacob. 1950. *The Customs Union Issue*. New York: Carnegie Endowment for International Peace.

Vollrath, Thomas L., and Charles B. Hallahan. 2011. *Reciprocal Trade Agreements: Impacts on Bilateral Trade Expansion and Contraction in the World Agricultural Marketplace*. Economic Research Report No. 113. U.S. Department of Agriculture, Economic Research Service, April, www.ers.usda.gov/publications/err113/

Vollrath, Thomas, Mark Gehlhar, and Charles Hallahan. 2009. "Bilateral Import Protection, Free Trade Agreements, and Other Factors Influencing Trade Flows in Agriculture and Clothing." *Journal of Agricultural Economics,* Vol. 60(2): 298-317, June.

Vollrath, Thomas, Charles Hallahan, and Mark Gehlhar. 2006. "Consumer Demand and Cost Factors Shape the Global Trade Network in Commodity and Manufactured Foods." *Canadian Journal of Agricultural Economics,* Vol. 54: 497-512, December, www3.interscience.wiley.com/ cgi-bin/fulltext/118594018/PDFSTART.

Wei, Shang-Jin, and Jeffrey A. Frankel. 1997. "Open Versus Closed Trade Blocs." In Takatoshi, Ito, and Anne O. Krueger (eds.), *Regionalism Versus Multilateral Trade Arrangements*. pp. 119-140. Chicago: The University of Chicago Press.

White, H. 1980. "A Heteroskedasticity-Consistent Covariance Matrix Estimator and a Direct Test for Heteroskedasticity." *Econometrica,* Vol. 48: 817-838.

Wooldridge, Jeffrey M. 2001. *Econometric Analysis of Cross Section and Panel Data*. Cambridge, MA: MIT Press.

World Bank. 2011. World Development Report 2011. http://wdronline.worldbank.org/?gclid=CJDizNn84qoCFcl95QodTEOj6g

___. 2008. *World Development Indicators, 2008.* www.worldbank.org/data/wdi2005/index.html.

World Trade Organization (WTO). 2011. "Regional Trade Agreements." http://rtais.wto.org/UI/PublicMaintainRTAHome.aspx.

___. 2008. "Tariff Escalation." *Working Document*, No. 11. Geneva, January.

___. 2000. "Synopsis of Systematic Issues Related to Regional Trade Agreements." Report by the Committee on Regional Trade Agreements. WTO Document WT/REG/E/37, March.

Zahniser, Steven S., Daniel Pick, Greg Pompelli, and Mark J. Gehlhar. 2004. "Trade Liberalization in the Western Hemisphere: Impacts on U.S. Agricultural Exports." In Mary E. Burfisher (ed.), *U.S. Agriculture and the Free Trade Area of the Americas*. Agricultural Economics Report No.

827, U.S. Department of Agriculture, Economic Research Service, March. www.ers.usda.gov/publications/aer827/

Appendix Table 1. Summary statistics for variables in the panel dataset

Variable	Mean	Std. deviation	Description
Xij_CF	53	(263)	Bulk commodity food trade between *i* and *j* (millions of U.S. dollars)
Xij_MF	131	(74)	Manufactured food exports by *i* to *j* (millions of U.S. dollars)
Yi	368	(1053)	Gross domestic product of importer *j* (billions of U.S. dollars)
Yj	362	(1055)	GDP of exporter *i* (billions of U.S. dollars)
EMij	5.19	(26)	Exchange-rate misalignment between *i* and *j*
FEij	23.85	(217)	Exporter-to-importer 0.1 hectare of arable land per worker in domestic labor force
DTij	7854	(4670)	Kilometers between the exporter *i* and importer *j*
CBij	0.0296	(0.1695)	Dummy: both countries share a common border
LLij	0.1243	(0.3299)	Dummy: If either or both countries are landlocked
LSij	0.2067	(0.4049)	Dummy: 9 percent or more of population in both countries sharing a common language
CHij	0.0144	(0.1192)	Dummy: existence of a colonial linkage after 1945
ITC^{ANDE}	0.0002	(0.0134)	Dummy: *i* and *j* in ANDE
XTC^{ANDE}	0.0091	(0.0947)	Dummy: *i* in ANDE, *j* outside of ANDE
MTD^{ANDE_US}	0.0002	(0.0133)	Dummy: U.S. as an exporter outside ANDE, *j* as an importer inside ANDE
$MTD^{ANDE\_non\text{-}US}$	0.0094	(0.0966)	Dummy: non-U.S. exporter outside ANDE, *j* as an importer inside ANDE
ITC^{ASEAN}	0.0014	(0.0373)	Dummy: *i* and *j* in ASEAN
XTC^{ASEAN}	0.0285	(0.1663)	Dummy: *i* in ASEAN, *j* outside of ASEAN
MTD^{ANSEAN_US}	0.0005	(0.0215)	Dummy: U.S. as an exporter outside ASEAN, *j* as an importer inside ASEAN
$MTD^{ASEAN\_non\text{-}US}$	0.0240	(0.1531)	Dummy: non-U.S. exporter outside ASEAN, *j* as an importer inside ASEAN
ITC^{CACM}	0.0027	(0.0517)	Dummy: *i* and *j* in CACM
XTC^{CACM}	0.0291	(0.1681)	Dummy: *i* in CACM, *j* outside of CACM
MTD^{CACM_US}	0.0007	(0.0259)	Dummy: U.S. as an exporter outside CACM, *j* as an importer inside CACM
$MTD^{CACM\_non\text{-}US}$	0.0271	(0.1623)	Dummy: non-U.S. exporter outside CACM, *j* as an importer inside CACM
ITC^{CER}	0.0004	(0.0202)	Dummy: *i* and *j* in CER
XTC^{CER}	0.0260	(0.1592)	Dummy: *i* in CER, *j* outside of CER
MTD^{CER_US}	0.0004	(0.0202)	Dummy: U.S. as an exporter outside CER, *j* as an importer inside CER
$MTD^{CER\_non\text{-}US}$	0.0234	(0.1512)	Dummy: non-U.S. exporter outside CER, *j* as an importer inside CER
ITC^{COMESA}	0.0005	(0.0225)	Dummy: *i* and *j* in COMESA
XTC^{COMESA}	0.0132	(0.1142)	Dummy: *i* in COMESA, *j* outside of COMESA

Variable	Mean	Std. deviation	Description
MTD^{COMESA_US}	0.0003	(0.0166)	Dummy: U.S. as an exporter outside COMESA, *j* as an importer inside COMESA
MTDCOMESA_non-US	0.0130	(0.1133)	Dummy: non-U.S. exporter outside COMESA, *j* as an importer inside COMESA
ITC^{EU}	0.0279	(0.1645)	Dummy: *i* and *j* in EU
XTC^{EU}	0.1615	(0.3679)	Dummy: *i* in EU, *j* outside of EU
MTD^{EU_US}	0.0028	(0.0531)	Dummy: U.S. as an exporter outside EU, *j* as an importer inside EU
$MTD^{EU\_non\text{-}US}$	0.1555	(0.3623)	Dummy: non-U.S. exporter outside EU, *j* as an importer inside EU
ITC^{GAFTA}	0.0019	(0.0435)	Dummy: *i* and *j* in GAFTA
XTC^{GAFTA}	0.0171	(0.1297)	Dummy: *i* in GAFTA, *j* outside of GAFTA
MTD^{GAFTA_US}	0.0004	(0.0207)	Dummy: U.S. as an exporter outside GAFTA, *j* as an importer inside GAFTA
$MTD^{GAFTA\_non\text{-}US}$	0.0217	(0.1457)	Dummy: non-U.S. exporter outside GAFTA, *j* as an importer inside GAFTA
ITC^{MERC}	0.0012	(0.0343)	Dummy: *i* and *j* in MERC
XTC^{MERC}	0.0216	(0.1455)	Dummy: *i* in MERC, *j* outside of MERC
MTD^{MERC_US}	0.0004	(0.0198)	Dummy: U.S. as an exporter outside MERC, *j* as an importer inside MERC
$MTD^{MERC\_non\text{-}US}$	0.0181	(0.1333)	Dummy: non-U.S. exporter outside MERC, *j* as an importer inside MERC
ITC^{NAFTA}	0.0007	(0.0270)	Dummy: *i* and *j* in NAFTA
XTC^{NAFTA}	0.0267	(0.1613)	Dummy: *i* in NAFTA, *j* outside of NAFTA
$MTD^{NAFTA\_non\text{-}US}$	0.0260	(0.1592)	Dummy: *i* outside of NAFTA, i inside NAFTA
ITC^{SADC}	0.0001	(0.0094)	Dummy: *i* and *j* in SADC
XTC^{SADC}	0.0042	(0.0644)	Dummy: *i* in SADC, *j* outside of SADC
MTD^{SADC_US}	0.0001	(0.0094)	Dummy: U.S. as an exporter outside SADC, *j* as an importer inside SADC
$MTD^{SADC\_non\text{-}US}$	0.0044	(0.0659)	Dummy: non-U.S. exporter outside SADC, *j* as an importer inside SADC
ITC^{SAPTA}	0.0011	(0.0325)	Dummy: *i* and *j* in SAPTA
XTC^{SAPTA}	0.0189	(0.1360)	Dummy: *i* in SAPTA, *j* outside of SAPTA
MTD^{SAPTA_US}	0.0004	(0.0189)	Dummy: U.S. as an exporter outside SAPTA, *j* as an importer inside SAPTA
$MTD^{SAPTA\_non\text{-}US}$	0.0166	(0.1278)	Dummy: non-U.S. exporter outside SAPTA, *j* as an importer inside SAPTA

End Notes

[1] The majority of gravity models focus on total merchandise trade. However, a growing number of applied studies published in recent years examine the impact of RTAs on agricultural trade (e.g., Zahniser et al., 2004; Clarete et al., 2003; Koo et al., 2006; Lambert and McKoy, 2009; Grant and Lambert, 2008; Jayasinghe and Sarker, 2008; and Vollrath et al., 2009).

[2] See Aitken, 1973; Sapir, 2001; Rose and van Wincoop, 2001; Cheng and Wall, 2005;Vollrath et al., 2006; Sandberg et al., 2006; Eicher and Henn, 2009; Subramanian and Wei, 2007; Baier and Bergstrand, 2007; and Baier et al., 2008.

[3] Viner (1950) was the first to define these terms.

[4] Studies addressing trade diversion include those that have deployed generic indexes from which generalizations can be drawn about the RTA phenomenon (e.g., Koo et al. 2006; Magee, 2008; and Vollrath and Hallahan, 2011) as well as those that have focused on specific RTAs, enabling distinctions to be made among individual agreements with different trade-policy orientations (Frankel, 1997; Frankel and Wei, 1997; Wei and Frankel, 1997; Endoh, 1999; Cernat, 2001; Tang, 2005; Grant and Lambert, 2005; and Sarker and Jayasinghe, 2007).

[5] To be more precise, data are needed on duties collected under most-favorednation (MFN) status and under preferential tariffs on imported goods from partner countries to assess the impact of RTAs on bilateral trade. Most countries simply do not provide public access to data on preferential tariffs.

[6] Panel data, unlike cross-sectional data, can disentangle time-specific from country- and partner-pair-specific effects.

[7] The 69 countries include Algeria, Argentina, Australia, Austria, Bangladesh, Belgium-Luxembourg, Brazil, Cameroon, Canada, Chile, China (mainland), Colombia, Costa Rica, Denmark, Dominican Republic, Egypt, El Salvador, Finland, France, Germany, Ghana, Greece, Guatemala, Honduras, Hong Kong, India, Indonesia, Ireland, Israel, Italy, Ivory Coast, Jamaica, Japan, Jordan, Kenya, Malaysia, Mexico, Morocco, Netherlands, New Zealand, Nicaragua, Nigeria, Norway, Pakistan, Panama, Paraguay, Philippines, Poland, Portugal, Saudi Arabia, Senegal, Singapore, South African Customs Union (Botswana, Lesotho, Namibia, South Africa, and Swaziland), South Korea, Spain, Sri Lanka, Sweden, Switzerland, Taiwan, Thailand, Trinidad-Tobago, Tunisia, Turkey, United Kingdom, United States, Uruguay, Venezuela, and Zambia.

[8] RTA-treatment effects relate to the partial effects of RTA-based binary variables on the continuous dependent variable, unidirectional trade flow. See Heckman (2001) and Wooldridge (2002). Countries signing an RTA are, for example, classified as the "treatment group," while country pairs that do not belong to the specific agreement are categorized as the "control group." Comparisons can then be drawn between the existing levels of partner trade that characterize the member countries trading with each other in the various RTAs to the hypothesized counterfactual levels in the absence of these agreements.

[9] In Linnemann's framework, markets cleared in response to the interaction between supply and demand forces, eliminating the need to include prices in applied analyses. His gravity model took the following reduced form: $X_{ij} = \beta_0 \frac{(s_i)^{\beta_1}(D_j)^{\beta_2}}{(R_{ij})^{\beta_3}}$ where X_{ij} denotes the volume of trade from country i and country j, s_i represents factors affecting the potential supply of the exporting country, D_j denotes factors affecting the potential demand of the importing country, and *Rij* consists of "resistance" factors that affect trade between the two countries, including impediments (such as transportation costs) as well as inducements (such as mutual RTA memberships).

[10] *EMijt* controls for the influence of current and accumulated experience: $EM_{ij} = V_t^1 + V_t^2 = \left[\frac{\max Z_{ij,t-k}^t - \min Z_{ij,t-k}^t}{\min Z_{ij,t-k}^t}\right] + \left[1 + \frac{\left|Z_{ij,t-k}^t - Z_{ij}^p\right|}{Z_{ij}^p}\right]^2$ where max (min) $Z_{ij,t-k}$ is the maximum (minimum) value of the exchange rate index over time interval of size k past period and Z_{ij}^p

is the mean of the exchange rate between 1975 and 2005. The central notion underlying $V_t^1$is that traders' uncertainty is conditioned by their memory of the high and low exchange rate over 10 years. V_t^2 puts the contemporaneous exchange rate into historical perspective. It captures nonlinear responses to departures of the current exchange rate from its longrun equilibrium rate.

[11] A reviewer suggested that we use an indicator of exchange-rate volatility rather than the exchange-rate misalignment variable. Others have noted that there is a certain amount of arbitrariness involved in choosing the appropriate exchange-rate variable to include in gravity models (Cho et al., 2002). We estimated the gravity models using Cho et al.'s measure of exchange-rate uncertainty in lieu of $EM_{ijt.}$ The empirical results using our exchange-rate misalignment indicator and Cho et al.'s variable (calculated as a moving standard deviation of the first differences in the bilateral exchange rate over the prior 10 years) were very similar. All the RTA parameter estimates carried the same signs and were nearly identical in magnitude. Both types of exchange-rate variables carried the same sign and were statistically significant at the 0.01 level. Our comparative results are available upon request.

[12] The 9-percent threshold serves to denote the level at which the ability to communicate is viewed as not imposing substantial transaction costs.

[13] $\alpha_t = 1$ when year is equal to t and 0 otherwise.

[14] The RTAs are coded dynamically. Hence, the NAFTA-related dummies take the value of 1 for the United States and Canada between 1989 and 2005 and for the United States and Mexico and Canada and Mexico between 1994 and 2005. Moreover, each RTA dummy was constructed using "full-year" enforcement, with full year referring to at least 8 months of agreement implementation.

[15] Lawrence (1996) notes that RTAs provide a vehicle for achieving deeper integration precisely because of their ability to remove and/or mitigate domestic barriers that inhibit cross-border trade.

[16] Note, cluster-robust standard errors are reported in parentheses in these tables using White's (1980) corrective method, rather than the default standard errors. Default standard errors, which assume *i.i.d.* errors, are likely to be underestimated because gravity models using panel data are subject to (1) positive autocorrelation within each bilateral pair over time as each additional observation is not providing information independently, and (2) heteroskedasticity because the composite error is likely to be correlated over time for a given country pair.

[17] Both the PA and FE estimators assume that the covariates are exogenous. They use *between* (cross-partner pairs) and *within* (time series) variation in the data. The RE model, by contrast, makes the strong assumption that the intercept is uncorrelated with the regressors. In contrast to the PA and RE models, the FE framework uses the *within* transformation. The transformation eliminates the αij's via centering. It permits arbitrary correlations between the omitted and the explanatory variables. This feature explains why the intercept varies over country pairs and over time in our generalized gravity equations.

[18] If the zeros are not randomly distributed, truncating the sample may generate a selection bias.

[19] Egger (2000) rejects the use of the RE estimator on both conceptual and empirical grounds in gravity models that are designed to gauge RTA treatment effects. He notes that in such models, "one is not interested in the estimation of typical trade flows between a randomly drawn sample of countries but between an *ex ante* predetermined selection of nations." Egger used the Hausman test to ompare the RE estimatr with th

[20] Convergence does not always occur with Poisson models because of estimator for a gravity model focus[ed]their "sensitivity to smll numerical on total merchandise trade [flows.]probles," ccording to pesonal His **empirical** test results **provide** communication from Santos Silva.

[21] The Ramsey RESET results for commodity and manufactured foods are not consistent with what Sun and Reed (2011) found when comparing OLS and Poisson models in their applied model for total agricultural trade.

[22] Our preferred PA benchmark models for food, though limited in their ability to diagnose the trade impacts of RTA, generate information about the fixed dyadic determinants that is not possible to obtain from the generalized models.

[23] The percentage change in trade attributable to RTA formation is $(e^{\delta^r} - 1)x100$.

[24] The formula to convert RTA coefficients into average annual percentage change is $\left(e^{\delta^r \frac{1}{n}} - 1\right)$, where n = the number of years the RTA is in force.

[25] There are a few instances where the gravity models generate negative MTD coefficients, but they are not statistically different from 0.

[26]As an example, one reviewer pointed out that MERCOSUR increased Argentine exports of wheat to Brazil while the United States lost share as Argentina now had the advantage of not paying the 10-percent "common external tariff."

[27] The three exceptions include the XTC^{CACM} coefficient that is significant at the .05-level in the bulk equation, which excludes the high-income RTAs and the $MTD^{ANDE\_non\text{-}US}$ and $MTD^{CACM\_non\text{-}US}$ coefficients that are insignificant in the manufactured food equation, which also excludes the high-income RTAs.

[28] Empirical results are available from the authors upon request.

[29] The United States promoted multilateral negotiations via the GATT during the 1960s and 1970s to counter discrimination inherent by the formation and expansion of the European Community (Bergsten, 1996). It is interesting that the concern about the erosion of exports by foreign suppliers due to the agreement uniting Europe proved to be prescient.

In: The Influence of Trade Agreements … ISBN: 978-1-62417-388-2
Editor: Benjamin Stenton

Chapter 2

RECIPROCAL TRADE AGREEMENTS: IMPACTS ON BILATERAL TRADE EXPANSION AND CONTRACTION IN THE WORLD AGRICULTURAL MARKETPLACE*

Thomas L. Vollrath and Charles B. Hallahan

ABSTRACT

The rapid increase in the number of bilateral and regional free-trade agreements since 1995 is a striking development. The proliferation of these agreements has raised questions about whether they have, in fact, opened markets, created trade, promoted economic growth, and/or distorted trade. This study uses panel data from 1975 to 2005 and a gravity framework model to identify the influence of reciprocal trade agreements (RTAs) on bilateral trade in the world agricultural marketplace. A benchmark, Heckman sample-selection and two generalized models, one of which accounts for RTA phase-in effects, are used to gauge the impact on partner trade of mutual as well as asymmetric RTA membership. Empirical results show that RTAs increase agricultural trade between member countries but decrease trade between member and nonmember countries. Interestingly, RTAs were

* This is an edited, reformatted and augmented version of United States Department of Agriculture, Economic Research Service, Economic Research Report Number 113, dated April 2011.

found to be particularly effective at expanding agricultural trade and opening markets in developing countries when developing-country trading partners are part of the same agreement.

SUMMARY

What Is the Issue?

Countries use bilateral/regional trade agreements to increase market access and expand trade in foreign markets. These agreements are called reciprocal trade agreements (RTAs) because members grant special advantages to each other. RTAs include many types of agreements, such as preferential arrangements, free trade agreements, customs unions, and common markets, in which members agree to open their markets to each other's exports by lowering trade barriers. They have become an increasingly prominent feature of the multilateral trading system in recent years, in part, because of stalled global negotiations taking place under the auspices of the World Trade Organization (WTO).

Many observers believe that RTAs deepen market integration and complement efforts by the WTO to liberalize international markets. While acknowledging that RTAs can open up markets, other observers contend that these agreements also distort trade and discriminate against nonmember countries.

Many studies have examined the degree to which RTAs increase trade between member countries. Relatively few, however, have attempted to quantify the extent to which RTAs curtail trade between member and nonmember countries. In this study, ERS empirically examines the bilateral trade expansion/contraction effects of RTAs in the world agricultural marketplace.

What Did the Study Find?

- Model results estimate that RTA membership boosts agricultural trade between member countries, on average, between 34 and 93 percent in the long run.
- The expansion of trade between RTA members typically comes at the expense of trade with nonmember countries. Empirical results show that agricultural trade falls, on average, between 26 and 46 percent in

the long run between two countries when one of them does not belong to an RTA to which the other is a member.

- The trade impacts of RTAs grow as producers and consumers adjust to policy-induced changes in market structure and as the implementing provisions of these agreements are phased in over time. Models that account for the cumulative, phase-in effects of RTAs show that, on average, agricultural trade increases 105 percent between two trading partners that belong to the same agreement in the long run but falls 49 percent between an RTA member country and a nonmember trading partner.
- RTAs boost trade in agricultural markets. The percentage increase in partner trade expansion induced by mutual RTA membership exceeds the percentage decline in partner trade characterizing asymmetric RTA membership.
- RTAs are particularly effective at expanding agricultural trade and opening markets in developing countries when both developing-country trading partners are members of the same agreement.

How Was the Study Conducted?

ERS developed econometric models to isolate the impacts of RTAs on bilateral trade in agriculture. Researchers adopted various approaches to control for the influence of the many factors affecting bilateral trade, such as the capacity of suppliers to export, the size of demand in importing countries, transaction costs, and characteristics that induce two countries to trade with each other (e.g., differences in resource endowments). The trade data deployed in model estimations included bilateral trade flows reported by UN Comtrade between 69 countries covering the 1975 to 2005 time frame. The empirical models identified statistical regularities, controlled for the unique institutional and physical characteristics of each country pair, and allowed for dynamic pricing and RTA phase-in effects. They yielded quantitative estimates of the impacts on partner trade of mutual and asymmetric RTA membership.

INTRODUCTION

Trade agreements, whether multilateral, regional, or bilateral in scope, are policy instruments that can increase market efficiency, expand trade, and enhance economic welfare of participant countries. Economists hold a particularly favorable view of the World Trade Organization (WTO), the global organization dealing with the rules of trade between nations, and its predecessor, the General Agreement on Tariffs and Trade (GATT). The GATT/WTO provides an international forum to supervise and liberalize trade worldwide and to ensure that trade flows as freely as possible. The guiding principle is open and free trade enunciated in the WTO's most-favored-nation (MFN) clause. The granting of MFN status means that a country should not discriminate among trading partners.

Acceptable rules and regulations of bilateral/regional trade agreements (RTAs) are identified in Article XXIV of the GATT/WTO. This Article establishes conditions governing cross-border barriers both within bilateral/regional trade agreements and between bilateral/regional-trade-agreement members and nonmembers. One condition eliminates or removes trade barriers on "substantially all the trade" within bilateral/regional trade agreements. Another prohibits member countries from raising trade barriers against nonmember countries above their pre-agreement levels.

Since the Annecy Round in 1949, the GATT/WTO has progressively reduced trade barriers in the world marketplace. Agriculture, however, was largely exempt from the trade-liberalizing rules that applied to most products under the GATT; that is, until the Uruguay Round Agricultural Agreement (URAA) in 1994. Still, many countries continue to use a variety of instruments to protect domestic agriculture and to curtail imports of agricultural goods in the post-URAA era. Examples include special safeguards, special and differential treatment for developing countries, relatively high tariffs, and comparatively modest access within tariff-rate quotas.

The Doha Round of the WTO was launched in 2001 with the aim of further opening up agricultural markets and increasing exporter access to both developed and developing country markets. However, no tangible breakthrough has been achieved after 9 years of negotiations. Stalled multilateral talks have provided opportunities for some countries to reduce trade barriers via reciprocal trade agreements (RTAs). These agreements arise when members agree to open their markets to each other's exports by lowering trade barriers. They can take various forms, such as preferential arrangements, free trade agreements, customs unions, and common markets.

RTAs have become an increasingly prominent feature of the multilateral trading system in recent years. According to the WTO, there were 186 such agreements in force in 2005, up from 50 just prior to the Uruguay Round in 1994, less than 25 in 1985, and just 13 agreements in 1975 (fig. 1).[1] As the number of agreements expanded, the RTA share of world trade rose from 22 percent in 1975 to over 50 percent in 2005.

Some economists believe that RTAs can be powerful forces promoting market liberalization that not only complement, but go beyond, multilateral trade efforts in the WTO to open international markets (Bergsten, 1998). While the WTO has progressively lowered tariffs worldwide, it has made little progress addressing other trade barriers, such as food safety concerns, domestic regulations, and incompatible technical standards. Harmonization of nontariff barriers is a source of trade and welfare gains of RTAs. For example, negotiations leading to the establishment of the North American Free Trade Agreement (NAFTA) addressed many contentious issues inhibiting trade. One result of these discussions was the removal import-licensing requirements for grapes in Mexico. The lifting of these requirements increased U.S. grape exports (Zahniser et al., 2004).

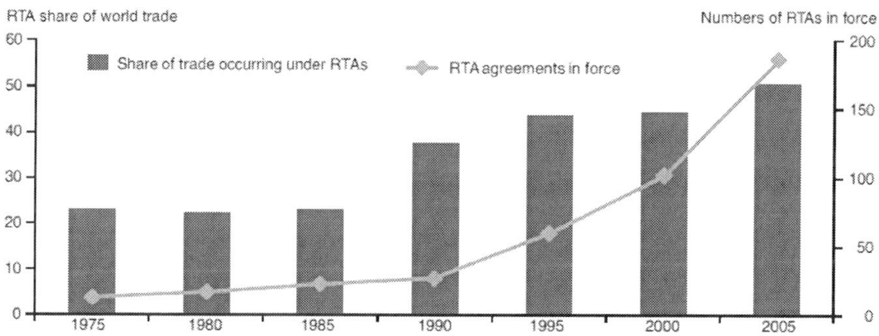

Source: USDA, Economic Research Service using Wainio (2006) and Grant and Lambert (2008b).

Figure 1. Growth in bilateral/regional trade agreements (RTAs) and their prominence in global markets.

Other economists are less convinced about the positive effects of bilateral/ regional trade agreements. They acknowledge that the formation and growth of RTAs can foster trade liberalization, deepen economic integration, and generate economic opportunities, but they also express concerns that these agreements can distort trade, increase discrimination against nonmember countries, and lower overall economic welfare (Bhagwati and Panagariya, 1996; Fiorentino et al., 2006).

Trade theory does not provide a definitive answer as to whether RTAs enhance economic welfare. Increases in partner trade of RTA members may be beneficial whenever production shifts toward the most efficient producers of specific goods within the trading bloc. Consumers are better off in countries belonging to a bilateral/regional trade agreement when they substitute lower priced imported goods from RTA partners for higher priced domestic goods. But while RTAs often increase trade among partner countries, they may also discriminate and favor relatively high-cost member-country suppliers at the expense of more efficient nonmember suppliers. The impacts of RTAs on the direction and flow of agricultural trade in the world marketplace depend not just upon trade expansion within member blocs but also on trade contraction between RTA and non-RTA members, a byproduct of these agreements. In this study, we empirically examine the effects on bilateral trade of RTAs in agriculture using Viner/Meade's notions of trade creation and trade diversion. According to Viner (1950), trade creation arises when RTAs induce shifts from domestic to partner country sources of supply. He posits that trade expansion occurs because low-cost products from producers in member countries displace high-cost domestic products. Trade diversion occurs, according to Viner, when RTAs trigger a shift in the source of production from nonmember suppliers to member countries. This happens when bloc partners reorient their imports away from low-cost, nonmember countries toward higher cost, member countries. Meade (1956) elaborated on Viner's production-oriented explanation to include RTA's effects on consumption. Meade points out that even if production in two countries belonging to the same RTA does not change, both countries may gain because lower prices enable their citizens to consume more of the goods for which they express a preference.

Applied research is needed to clarify the economic tradeoffs of bilateral/regional trade agreements. To date, most econometric studies have focused on quantifying the extent to which mutual RTA membership has expanded trade. Relatively few studies have examined how asymmetric RTA membership may also have lowered trade. In this study, the primary objective of ERS is to empirically examine the impacts of RTAs on bilateral trade in agriculture where restrictive domestic and border policies continue to pose significant impediments to free and open trade. We use the gravity framework and panel data to quantify the degree to which these agreements have affected partner trade, both positively and negatively.

ECONOMETRIC MODELS

Clearly, many economic forces besides the establishment of bilateral/regional free-trade agreements shape the direction and volume of trade in the global market. When attempting to empirically isolate the ex-post impact of RTAs, it is, therefore, important to control for the many other determinants affecting partner trade. The gravity framework, which can account for myriad influences, is well suited to identify how these agreements shape cross-border trade.[2] See the appendix for a summary of advances in applied analyses and theoretical linkages underlying the gravity framework.

The gravity framework has been widely used in applied research to assess the RTA impacts on trade between member countries. For example, the following studies have deployed the commonly used RTA dummy variable—defined as equaling one when both the exporter and importer are members of the same agreement, and zero otherwise: Aitken, 1973; Sapir, 2001; Rose and van Wincoop, 2001; Cheng and Wall, 2005; Vollrath et al., 2006; Sandberg et al., 2006; Eicher and Henn, 2009; Subramanian and Wei, 2007; Baier and Bergstrand, 2007; Baier et al., 2008; Grant and Lambert, 2008a.

Soloaga and Winters (2001) developed a model designed to control for relative openness of RTA member countries with the objective of removing the potential bias in intrabloc coefficients. The gravity equations used in their study (as well as in studies by Clarete et al., 2003, and Lambert and McKoy, 2009) include dummy variables to denote mutual RTA membership as well as two dummy variables to control for systematic openness of RTA members, one for the exporter and one for the importer. The *exporter openness* dummy equals one should the exporter be a member of a designated RTA regardless of the status of the importing country. The *importer openness* dummy is defined similarly. It equals one should the importing country belong to an RTA, regardless of the status of the exporting country.

In addition to estimating the intrabloc effects on unidirectional trade flows, applied research has been used to determine whether trade agreements increase two-way trade, advance trade liberalization, and/or lead to market distortions. Eichengreen and Irwin (1995); Bayoumi and Eichengreen (1997); Wei and Frankel (1997); and Ghosh and Yamarik (2004) sought to determine whether individual RTAs were *open* or *closed* trading blocs in models where the dependent variable was the "sum of exports and imports." Rose (2004) and Tomz et al. (2007) addressed whether trade agreements increase the "average value of bilateral trade," using dummy variables to denote mutual membership in these agreements. Vicard (2009) examined whether different types of RTAs (i.e., preferential arrangements, free trade agreements, custom unions, and common markets) affect "total bilateral trade" differentially.

Several studies have developed models designed explicitly to estimate both trade creation and trade diversion. Endoh (1999) developed a model that focused on the European Economic Community, the Latin American Free Trade Association, and the Council of Mutual Economic Assistance. Tang (2005) directed attention to NAFTA, the Closer Economic Relations trade agreement between Australia and New Zealand, and the Association of Southeast Asian Nations (ASEAN) trade agreement. Koo et al. (2006) focused attention on the European Union, NAFTA, the ASEAN, and the Andean Community. Magee (2008) and Vollrath et al. (2009) developed generic indexes to quantify overall trade creation and trade diversion. All of the gravity model studies enumerated here, with the exception of Tang and Magee, were estimated using cross-sectional data.[3]

The use of panel, rather than cross-sectional data, is generally preferred, especially in a gravity model incorporating RTA dummy variables. In cross-sectional estimates, the RTA dummies account for everything specific to the bilateral pairs not captured by the invariant fixed effects (e.g., distance) specified in the model. As a result, the RTA dummies in such models do not really isolate the trade-creation and trade-diversion effects. Panel-based models also offer a better opportunity to account for changes (e.g., changes in income) taking place within and between countries over time. Moreover, they generate more efficient parameter estimates. Importantly, they enable the researcher to enrich model specification with fixed effects that mitigate omitted-variable and heterogeneity bias, which more effectively isolates the impacts of RTAs.

In this study, ERS uses panel data and information about mutual and asymmetric RTA membership to estimate gravity models that contain generic RTA indices designed to approximate Viner/Meade's trade creation and trade diversion effects in the global marketplace.[4] The binary mutual-agreement index (*MA*) takes a value of one whenever two countries jointly belong to the same RTA, otherwise *MA* equals zero. The asymmetric-agreement index (*AA*) takes a value of one whenever the exporter is not a member of an RTA to which the importer belongs and zero otherwise. A positive and statistically significant *MA* coefficient indicates that bilateral trade between two countries belonging to the same RTA increases as a result of the removal of tariffs and nontariff restrictions. A negative and significant *AA* coefficient indicates that imports by an RTA member from a nonmember falls as a result of asymmetric membership.

MA and *AA* capture, respectively, bilateral trade expansion and trade contraction in the global marketplace due to RTAs. They do not measure the welfare effects of these agreements, for such effects depend not only on the amount of trade created and diverted but also on relative efficiencies or differences in unit costs. As noted in Palgrave (1987), trade creation increases economic welfare when higher cost domestic sources of supply are replaced by lower cost imports from partner countries that had been constrained by tariffs and nontariff barriers. Trade diversion has a welfare cost when trade-policy discrimination against nonmember countries leads to the replacement of lower cost sources of supply in these countries by higher cost partner country sources.

We estimate two conventional and two generalized gravity models using fixed effects.[5] The conventional models are based upon commonly used benchmark equations as well as Heckman's sample-selection framework. The generalized models are structured to conform to Anderson and van Wincoop's (2003; 2004) analytical framework. The first generalized model is a dummy-intensive fixed-effects model that incorporates exporter-by-time, importer-by-time, and export-import pair dummies. The second includes the same set of fixed effects as the first, but adds RTA phase-in variables to complement the contemporaneous RTA variable. To address the issue of heterogeneity of partner trade, we ran the generalized model not only on the global sample of bilateral trade flows between 69 countries but also on eight subsamples, consisting of various combinations of developed and developing countries exporting and importing from each other.

The Benchmark Model

The basic gravity framework using panel data relates exports by country i to country j in year t to the market size of both countries in year t and economic distance or trade costs separating the two countries. In our conventional gravity models, we follow the literature and use Gross Domestic Product (GDP) to quantify market size. The time-varying GDP of the exporting country, (Y_{it}), represents the potential supply of goods from that country. The GDP of the importing country, (Y_{jt}), reflects the potential demand of the goods being traded.[6] Since data on trade costs are not readily available, our basic model includes observable variables to reflect different aspects of bilateral trade costs, namely transportation costs, cultural proximity, and partner trade policies.

Our benchmark gravity equation takes the following form:

$$\ln(X_{ijt}) = \alpha_0 + \gamma_t + \alpha_1 \ln(Y_{it}) + \alpha_2 \ln(Y_{jt}) + \beta_1 \ln(FE_{ijt}) + \beta_2 \ln(DT_{ij}) + \beta_3 (CB_{ij}) + \beta_4 (LL_{ij}) + \beta_5 (LS_{ij}) + \beta_6 (CH_{ij}) + \beta_7 (TP_{ijt}) + \varepsilon_{ijt} \quad (1)$$

factor endowments are captured by (FE_{ijt}), a measure of exporter-to-importer arable-land/total-labor ratios in year *t*. The indicators for transportation costs include physical distance (DT_{ij}) and two dummy variables to reflect geographical adjacency, (CB_{ij}) which equals 1 when *i* and *j* share a contiguous border and 0 otherwise and landlockedness (LL_{ij}), which equals 1 when either *i* or *j* are landlocked and 0 otherwise. The measures for cultural proximity include language similarity (LS_{ij}) a dummy variable which equals 1 whenever 9 percent or more of the population in both countries share a common language and 0 otherwise;[7] and colonial heritage (CH_{ij}), a dummy variable which equals 1 if two countries have established colonial ties since 1945 and 0 otherwise.[8] Time dummies (γ_t) account for factors common to all countries, including worldwide inflation, increases in trade attributable to globalization, and general shocks affecting the world economy.[9] We include two dummy variables to represent domestic trade policies (TP_{ijt}) in each model type: (1) a dummy variable denoting mutual membership in RTAs (MA_{ijt}), which equals 1 in year *t* when two trading partners are both members of the same bilateral/regional trade agreement and 0 otherwise; and/or (2) a dummy variable denoting asymmetric membership in these agreements (AA_{ijt}), which equals 1 in year *t* when *i* is not a member of an RTA to which *j* belongs and 0 otherwise.[10]

Most gravity models are specified in log-linear terms because of ease of calculation and interpretation. This specification is not, however, without its problems. Taking logarithms often removes observations from the sample because the log of zero is undefined. Omitting zero-flow or missing observations implies that information is lost on the causes of no or very low trade. Moreover, the practice of dropping observations may produce downwardly biased and inconsistent parameter estimates. Consequently, the dependent variable in gravity models estimated using samples where no trade is recorded for some export-to-import partners is no longer bilateral trade; rather, it is bilateral trade contingent on the existence of trading relationships.

The Heckman Model

Heckman's (1979) sample-selection model offers a theoretically sound and econometrically elegant way to include zero flows in models of bilateral trade (Linders and de Groot, 2006).[11] The sample selection gravity model allows for the correlation between (1) the joint decision of whether *i* chooses to export to *j* and *j* chooses to import from *i* and (2) the amount, if any, of unidirectional trade between i and j. In other words, this model accounts for the relationship between *expected profitability* and *conditional expected trade*. A "selection equation" is used to incorporate the binary decision of whether or not to trade based on expected profitability. Then, an "outcome equation" determines the volume of bilateral trade.

To circumvent problems associated with zero trade flows, we estimate conventional gravity equations using Heckman's sample-selection framework. We chose the maximum likelihood estimator (MLE), as research has shown that MLE is preferred over the Heckman two-step estimator to jointly estimate the selection and outcome equations (Martin and Pham, 2008).

Formally, the Heckman model distinguishes between the selection and outcome processes:

$$s^*_{ij} = z_{ij}\delta + v_{ij} \text{ (selection mechanism)}$$

$$y_{ij} = x_{ij}\beta + \mu_{ij} \text{(outcome mechanism)}$$

where z_{ij} and x_{ij} are the vectors of variables affecting the selection and outcome mechanisms, respectively; s^* is the underlying latent variable representing the decision whether to trade (s is observed to be 1 if trade occurs and 0 otherwise); y is the log of trade when trade occurs ($s = 1$); and the μ and v errors are assumed to be jointly normally distributed with correlation p.

The expected value of y, given that it is observed, is

$$E[\, y \mid \boldsymbol{s} = 1\,] = \boldsymbol{x\beta} + p\lambda\boldsymbol{(z\delta)}$$

where $\lambda\boldsymbol{(z\delta)}$ is the Inverse Mills Ratio (IMR).[12]

The first set of covariates in the sample-selection model determine the probability of whether the two countries engage in trade. The second set of covariates determines the intensity of bilateral trade, conditional on the existence of a trade relationship. MLE estimation allows for the probability of trade and the size of potential trade to be explained jointly.

Our sample-selection model for bilateral agricultural trade is specified as follows:

The selection equation

$$s^*_{ijt} = \delta_0 + \delta_t + \delta_1 \ln(Y_{it}) + \delta_2 \ln(Y_{jt}) + \delta_3 (FE_{ijt}) + \delta_4 \ln(D_{ij}) + \delta_5 \ln(CB_{ij})$$
$$+ \delta_6 \ln(LL_{ij}) + \delta_7 \ln(LS_{ij}) + \delta_8 (CH_{ij}) + \delta_9 (TP_{ijt}) + \upsilon_{ijt} \qquad (2)$$

where

$$s_{ijt} = 1 \text{ if } s^*_{ijt} > 0$$

$$s_{ijt} = 0 \text{ if } s^*_{ijt} \leq 0$$

The outcome equation[13]

$$\ln(X^*_{ijt}) = \beta_0 + \beta_t + \beta_1 \ln(Y_{it}) + \beta_2 \ln(Y_{jt}) + +\beta_3 \ln(FE_{ijt}) + \beta_4 \ln(D_{ij}) + \beta_5 \ln(CB_{ij}) + \beta_6 \ln(LL_{ij}) + \beta_7 (CH_{ij}) + \beta_8 (TP_{ijt}) + \mu_{ijt} \quad (3)$$

where

$$(\mu_{ijt}, v_{ijt}) - \text{bivariate normal} \left[0, 0, 1, \sigma^2_{\upsilon}, \rho_{v\mu}\right]$$

The Generalized Gravity Models

Anderson and van Wincoop (AvW) developed a generalized gravity model in which prices play a central equilibrating role. Baier and Bergstrand (BB) extended the AvW framework to a panel setting and estimated models that controlled for the effects of changes in multilateral prices through time via the use of exporter-by-time and importer-by-time fixed effects. BB's generalized gravity model also controls for partner heterogeneity via the use of exporter-to-importer fixed effects. These country-pair dummies account for the whole host of time-invariant dyadic determinants (e.g., the special relationship established between Japan and the United States) that mutually affect the volume of trade for each partner pair. Baier and Bergstrand also developed a model that includes RTA lags in order to gauge the phase-in effects of these agreements on member countries' trade over time.

Generalized gravity models address the concerns about proper specification identified earlier. Following AvW and BB, the first such model we estimate is as follows:

$$\ln(X_{ijt}) = \alpha_0 + \gamma_{ij} + \gamma_{it} + \gamma_{jt} + \beta_1(TP_{ijt}) + \varepsilon_{ijt} \quad (4)$$

where γ_{it} denotes exporter-by-time fixed effects, γ_{jt} signifies importer-by-time fixed effects, and γ_{ij} represents exporter-to-importer fixed effects.[14] Equation (4) does not include either $\ln(Y_{it})$ or $\ln(Y_{it})$, as these regressors are absorbed by γ_{it} and γ_{it}, respectively. Similarly, specific dyadic variables, such as distance and contiguity, are absorbed by γij.

Equation (4) overcomes many of the shortcomings of conventional gravity models. The country-by-time dummies control for multilateral resistances á la AvW. These dummies not only account for time-varying export and import price indexes that influence bilateral trading decisions but also sweep away country-specific time-varying effects, such as shifts in domestic policies and macroeconomic shocks. The exporter-to-importer dummies provide a way to more thoroughly control for cultural and physical heterogeneity among country pairs than determinants commonly found in conventional gravity models (e.g., distance, contiguity, language similarity, and common colonial heritage).

RTAs typically take time to mature. Their effects on trade cannot, therefore, be completely captured with binary variables using the date RTAs entered into force. The second generalized model we estimate follows Baier and Bergstrand's framework and incorporates lagged RTA dummies to address this problem. This framework includes the same set of fixed effects as the first, but adds RTA phase-in variables.

Our RTA phase-in model includes contemporaneous and lagged RTA dummy variables at 5 and 10 years as follows:

$$\ln(X_{ijt}) = \alpha_0 + \gamma_{ij} + \gamma_{it} + \gamma_{jt} + \varphi_1(TP_{ij,t}) + \varphi_2(TP_{ij,t-5}) + \varphi_3(TP_{ij,t-10}) + \varepsilon_{ijt} \quad (5)$$

The lagged variables mitigate measurement errors typically found in gravity models that include RTAs as explanatory variables that arise due to the inability of contemporaneous 0-1 dummy variables to account for the phase-in effects of these agreements. In recognition of heterogeneity characterizing partner trade, equation (5) was run not only on the global sample of 69 countries trading with each other but also on 8 subsamples, categorized by various combinations of high and low per capita incomes of the exporting and importing countries.

DATA

The panel dataset developed for this study includes bilateral trade flows for agriculture among 69 countries at 5-year intervals beginning in 1975 and ending in 2005.[15] Most, but not all, countries export (import) to every other country. However, 20 percent of the cells are "missing" in the agricultural trade matrix.[16] Summary statistics for the variables in the panel dataset are shown in table 1.

Bilateral trade data were obtained from the United Nations Commodity Trade Statistics (UN Statistical Office, 2008) database, *UN Comtrade*, the primary international data source for partner- and product-specific trade that includes most countries and products. The WTO's definition of agriculture is used to quantify total agricultural trade. Distances between capital cities and/ or the major commercial center closest to partner countries were calculated using the great circle method obtained from USDA's Agricultural Research Service. Data on colonial heritage and landlockedness were obtained from Andrew Rose's (2006) website. Data on language similarity were obtained from the Centre d'Etudes Prospectives et d'Informations Internationales (2005) website. Information about arable land was obtained from the United Nations Food and Agricultural Organization's (2008) FAOSTAT database. Data on bilateral/regional trade agreements and their date of entry into force were compiled by scrutinizing multiple sources, including Oh (2006) and the WTO website (see box, "MA and AA: Two Generic RTA Variables Denoting Bilateral Trade Policies"). All other data were obtained from *World Development Indicators* (see World Bank, 2005).

MA and AA: Two Generic RTA Variables Denoting Bilateral Trade Policies

The proliferation of bilateral and regional trade agreements in recent years raises the question of the impact of this phenomenon on agricultural trade in the world marketplace. This study examines this phenomenon and gauges its impact on partner trade in cases of mutual and asymmetric RTA membership using two generic indices. The MA index is used to quantify trade creation characterizing joint RTA membership. The AA index is used to compute trade diversion typifying partners when the exporter is not a member of an RTA to which the importer belongs.

Both measures incorporate the following reciprocal preferential arrangements, free-trade agreements, customs unions, and common markets: Andean Community, Association of Southeast Asian Nations (ASEAN), Australia-Singapore Agreement, Australia-Thailand Agreement, Canada-Chile Agreement, Canada-Costa Rica Agreement, Canada-Israel Agreement, Canada-U.S. Free Trade Agreement, Caribbean Community, Central American Common Market, Chile-Costa Rica Agreement, Chile-El Salvador Agreement, Chile-Israel Agreement, China-Hong Kong Agreement, Closer Economic Relations, Common Market for Eastern and Southern Africa, European Free Trade Agreement (EFTA), EFTA-Chile Agreement, EFTA-Israel Agreement, EFTA-Jordan Agreement, EFTA-Mexico Agreement, EFTA-Morocco Agreement, EFTA-Poland Agreement, EFTA-Singapore Agreement, EFTA-Turkey Agreement, European Union (EU), EU-Algeria Agreement, EU-Chile Agreement, EU-Egypt Agreement, EU-Israel Agreement, EU-Jordan Agreement, EU-Mexico Agreement, EU-Morocco Agreement, EU-Norway Agreement, EU-South Africa Agreement, EU-Switzerland Agreement, EU-Tunisia Agreement, EU-Turkey Agreement, G-3 Free Trade Area, Greater Arab Free Trade Area, Gulf Cooperation Council, India-Sri Lanka Agreement, Japan-Singapore Agreement, Latin American Integration Agreement, MERCOSUR, MERCOSUR-Chile Agreement, Mexico-Chile Agreement, Mexico-Costa Rica Agreement, Mexico-El Salvador Agreement, Mexico-Guatemala Agreement, Mexico-Honduras Agreement, Mexico-Israel Agreement, Mexico-Japan Agreement, Mexico-Nicaragua Agreement, New Zealand-Singapore Agreement, North American Free Trade Agreement, Panama-El Salvador Agreement, Poland-Israel Agreement, Poland-Turkey Agreement, South African Development Community, South Asian Preferential Trade Arrangement, Turkey-Israel Agreement, U.S.-Australia Free Trade Agreement, U.S.-Chile Free Trade Agreement, U.S.-Israel Free Trade Agreement, U.S.-Jordan Free Trade Agreement, and the U.S.-Singapore Free Trade Agreement.

Table 1. Summary statistics for variables in panel dataset

Variable	Statistics[1]	Description
Xij	70 (355)	Agricultural trade between i and j (millions of U.S. dollars)
Yi	377 (1,105)	GDP of exporter i (billions of U.S. dollars)

Table 1. (Continued)

Variable	Statistics[1]	Description
Yj	370 (1,105)	GDP of importer j (billions of U.S. dollars)
FEij	24 (218)	Relative factor endowment: exporter-to-importer 0.1 hectare of arable land per worker in the total labor force
DTij	7,910 (4,666)	Kilometers between exporter i's and importer j's major commercial cities
CBij	0.03 (0.17)	Dummy: both countries share a common border
LLij	0.13 (0.33)	Dummy: if either or both countries are landlocked
LSij	0.21 (0.41)	Dummy: 9 percent or more of the population in both countries share a common language
CHij	0.01 (0.12)	Dummy: existence of a colonial linkage after 1945
MAij	0.10 (0.29)	Dummy: mutual RTA membership
AAij	0.90 (0.30)	Dummy: asymmetric RTA membership
No. of observations	25,931	

[1] Sample means with standard deviations in parentheses.
Source: USDA, Economic Research Service.

EMPIRICAL FINDINGS

Econometric results for the applied gravity models are displayed in tables 2-6. Tables 2 and 3 contain the statistical results for the benchmark and Heckman models.

Table 4 presents empirical findings from the dummy-intensive generalized model focused on contemporaneous RTA variables.

Tables 5 and 6 exhibit statistics from the generalized-gravity models that account for contemporaneous as well as RTA phase-in effects.

Findings from Benchmark and Heckman Models

Most parameter estimates in the benchmark models and the Heckman output equations are similar in magnitude and statistical significance (tables 2 and 3).[17] The size of the exporter-income, importer-income, and factor-endowment coefficients are virtually identical and statistically significant at the 0.01 level in both models. Interestingly, the absolute size of the coefficients for distance, common border, landlockedness, and colonial heritage are slightly smaller in the benchmark than in the Heckman models. By contrast, the *MA* and *AA* parameter estimates are somewhat larger. Given that incidental truncation was found to characterize agricultural trade in the sample-selection model, these results are not surprising.[18] They point to parameter bias in log-linear models due to omitted observations.[19] This bias is not, however, severe.

Both models generated correct signs for the basic gravity variables, income and distance. The magnitude of the parameter estimates for these two determinants fall within conventionally acceptable levels. The statistically significant distance elasticities equal -0.78 in the benchmark models and -0.84 in the outcome equations of the sample-selection model. The generated income elasticities with respect to agricultural trade range from 0.71 for exporters to 0.79 for importers. The higher elasticity for imports is not unexpected given the relatively high demand for food in the developing countries.

The factor-endowment elasticity with respect to agricultural trade equals 0.18. The finding of a positive parameter estimate for the exporter-to-importer land/labor ratio shows that national resources are an important determinant of cross-border trade in agriculture. It provides empirical validation of the relevance of economic trade theory and the Heckscher-Ohlin (H-O) explanation of trade. H-O theory leads one to expect that the uni-directional flow of agricultural trade from *i* and *j* would be positively related to the relative land/labor ratio because the production of agricultural goods requires relative intensive use of arable land.

Coefficients for the invariant dyadic variables—landlockedness, common borders, language similarity, and colonial heritage—are statistically significant at the 0.01 level, and each has the hypothesized sign in tables 2 and 3. The cost to trade whenever either the exporter or the importer is landlocked imposes an ad valorem tax equivalent of 4 to 10 percent, given parameter estimates in the benchmark and Heckman models and the assumption that the elasticities of substitution range between 5 and 10.[20] Sharing a common border generates a competitive trade advantage for contiguous partners, providing them effectively with an ad valorem subsidy equivalent between 0.07 and 0.20 percent. However, contiguity was found not to affect the decision to trade in the selection equations.

Table 2. Benchmark gravity model (OLS)

		Coeffi cients		
Variables	Symbols	MA and AA	MA only	AA only
Exporter's income	ln(Yi)	0.71**	0.71**	0.71**
		(0.01)	(0.01)	(0.01)
		0.79**	0.79**	0.79**
Importer's income	ln(Yj)	(0.01)	(0.01)	(0.01)
		0.18**	0.18**	0.18**
Relative land/labor	ln(FEij)	(0.01)	(0.01)	(0.01)
		-0.78**	-0.78**	-0.78**
Distance	ln(DT_{ij})	(0.02)	(0.02)	(0.02)
		0.59**	0.59**	0.59**
Common border	CBij	(0.08)	(0.08)	(0.08)
		-0.41**	-0.40**	-0.40**
Landlockedness	LLij	(0.04)	(0.04)	(0.04)
		0.62**	0.62**	0.62**
Language similarity	LSij	(0.04)	(0.04)	(0.04)
		1.43**	1.43**	1.42**
Colonial heritage	CHij	(0.09)	(0.09)	(0.09)
		0.82**	0.66**	
Mutual RTA membership	MAij	(0.24)	(0.05)	
		0.16		-0.61**
Asymmetrical RTA membership	AAij	(0.24)		(0.05)
		15.49**	15.64**	16.30**
Constant	C	(0.29)	(0.18)	(0.16)
Adjusted R^2		0.446	0.446	0.446
F-statistic		1,754	1,871	1,852
Root MSE		2.341	2.341	2.341
No. of observations		25,931	25,931	25,931

Notes: The dependent variable is the natural log of agricultural bilateral trade $_{(\ln X_{ijt})}$ from country *i* to country *j* in year *t*. RTA = reciprocal trade agreement. MA = mutual-agreement index. AA = Asymmetric-agreement index. All regressions are estimated using 5-year panel data from 1975 to 2005. Coefficient estimates for the fixed time effects are not reported for brevity. Standard errors are in parentheses. They are calculated using White's heteroskedastic robust standard errors.

** denotes the null hypothesis is rejected at the 0.01 level.

Source: USDA, Economic Research Service.

Table 3. Heckman's sample selection model (MLE)

		Coeffi cients					
		MA and AA		MA only		AA only	
Variables	Symbols	Outcome	Selection	Outcome	Selection	Outcome	Selection
Exporter's income	ln(Yi)	0.71** (0.01)	0.42** (0.01)	0.71** (0.01)	0.42** (0.01)	0.71** (0.01)	0.42** (0.01)

		Coeffi cients					
		MA and AA		MA only		AA only	
Variables	Symbols	Outcome	Selection	Outcome	Selection	Outcome	Selection
		0.79**	0.31**	0.79**	0.31**	0.79**	0.31**
Importer's income	ln(Yj)	(0.01)	(0.01)	(0.01)	(0.01)	(0.01)	(0.01)
		0.18**	0.00	0.18**	0.00	0.18**	0.00
Relative land/labor	ln(FEij)	(0.01)	(0.00)	(0.01)	(0.00)	(0.01)	(0.00)
		-0.84**	-0.38**	-0.84**	-0.39**	-0.84**	-0.38**
Distance	$\ln(DT_{ij})$	(0.02)	(0.02)	(0.02)	(0.02)	(0.02)	(0.02)
		0.77**	-0.08	0.77**	-0.08	0.78**	-0.08
Common border	CBij	(0.08)	(0.12)	(0.08)	(0.12)	(0.08)	(0.12)
		-0.42**	0.05*	-0.42**	0.05*	-0.42**	0.05*
Landlockedness	LLij	(0.04)	(0.02)	(0.04)	(0.02)	(0.04)	(0.02)
			0.13**		0.13**		0.13**
Language similarity	LSij		(0.02)		(0.02)		(0.02)
		1.79**	5.86**	1.79**	5.85**	1.79**	5.84**
Colonial heritage	CHij	(0.09)	(0.06)	(0.09)	(0.06)	(0.09)	(0.06)
		0.79**	0.12	0.61**	0.52**		
Mutual RTA membership	MAij	(0.24)	(0.32)	(0.05)	(0.10)		
		0.19	-0.42			-0.56**	-0.52**
Asymmetrical RTA membership	AAij	(0.24)	(0.30)			(0.05)	(0.10)
		16.08**	2.51**	16.25**	2.10**	16.87**	2.61**
Constant	C	(0.29)	(0.33)	(0.18)	(0.15)	(0.17)	(0.16)
No. of observations		32,572	32,572	32,572	32,572	32,572	32,572
Censored observations		6,641	6,641	6,641	6,641	6,641	6,641
Log likelihood		-70,770	-70,770	-70,772	-70,772	-70,777	-70,777
Wald-statistic		30,454	30,454	30,494	30,494	30,398	30,398
rho	P_{μ}	0.06	0.06	0.06	0.06	0.07	0.07
sigma	σ	2.35	2.35	2.35	2.35	2.35	2.35
lambda	λ	0.15	0.15	0.15	0.15	0.16	0.16

Notes: The dependent variable is the natural log of agricultural bilateral trade $(\ln X_{ijt})$ from country *i* to country *j* in year *t*. RTA = reciprocal trade agreement. MA = mutual-agreement index. AA = Asymmetric-agreement index. All regressions are estimated using 5-year panel data from 1975 to 2005. Coefficient estimates for the fixed time effects are not reported for brevity. Standard errors are in parentheses. They are calculated using White's heteroskedastic robust standard errors. ** denotes the null hypothesis is rejected at the 0.01 level.

Source: USDA, Economic Research Service.

The empirical results show that "cultural distances" matter. Language similarity and colonial heritage have the expected positive sign and are significant at the 1-percent level in the agricultural sector. The ability of a significant proportion of the population in both countries to communicate in the same language increases trade relative to other countries between 0.6 and 0.9 percent, on average. Possession of a colonial heritage also affects the decision to trade. Given an affirmative decision to trade, the colonial linkage augments bilateral trade in agriculture between 3 and 5 percent.

The benchmark and sample-selection models generated trade policy parameters that are similar in magnitude and statistical significance for each of the three specifications. The models that include both *MA* and *AA* variables provided statistical evidence that RTAs expand trade between member countries but no evidence that these agreements contract trade from nonmembers.

However, given the high correlation between the two trade-policy variables, multicollinearity causes difficulty in identifying the separate effects of *MA* and *AA*. We, therefore, ran separate equations, one excluding the mutual-agreement and the other excluding the asymmetric-agreement variables. Dropping one of the trade policy variables generated parameter estimates of the anticipated correct signs that were statistically significant at the 0.01 level. More specifically, the *MA* coefficients fell from 0.82 (0.79) in the *MA* and *AA* specification to 0.66 (0.61) in the *MA*-only benchmark (sample-selection) model. In addition, the *AA* coefficients became statistically significant in the two TD-only models, equaling -0.61 in the benchmark and -0.56 in the sample-selection models.

The long-run increase in RTA-induced trade between countries mutually belonging to the same agreements was found, on average, to outpace the fall in trade characterized by asymmetric membership. Results from the *MA*-only models show that, on average, mutual RTA membership enhances partner trade in agriculture between 93 and 84 percent for the benchmark and Heckman models, respectively.[21] Similarly, estimates from the *AA*-only models indicate that asymmetrical RTA membership lowers bilateral trade between 46 and 43 percent when the importer is a member of an RTA to which the exporter does not belong.

Findings from the Generalized Models

The *MA* and *AA* coefficients were not statistically significant in the contemporaneous generalized gravity model when both trade-policy variables were included in the estimating equation (table 4, column 1). However, upon purging the equations of severe multicollinearity via the removal of either the *MA* or *AA* variable, the parameter estimates for both trade-policy variables became statistically significant at the 0.01 level and were of the correct sign (table 4, column 2 & 3). Interestingly, the 0.29 coefficient for *MA* and the -0.30 coefficient for AA are less than half the size of corresponding estimates in tables 2 and 3. The lower parameter estimates for the trade-policy variables indicate that the longrun percentage increase (decrease) in agricultural trade due to common (asymmetric) RTA membership is, on average, 34 (26) percent. The smaller RTA impacts generated by the generalized model are due to more comprehensive control of both observed and unobserved heterogeneity than in either the benchmark or Heckman models.[22]

Table 4. Generalized gravity model

	Coeffi cients			
Variables	Symbols	MA and AA	MA only	AA only
Mutual RTA membership	MAij	0.09 (0.15)	0.29** (0.05)	
Asymmetrical RTA membership	AAij	-0.22 (0.16)		-0.30** (0.05)
Constant	C	14.11** (0.17)	12.85** (0.42)	13.48** (0.38)
Adjusted R^2		0.84	0.84	0.84
F-statistic		19.04	19.04	19.04
Root MSE		1.28	1.28	1.28
No. of observations		26,114	26,114	26,114

Notes: The dependent variable is the natural log bilateral trade $_{(\ln X_{ijt})}$ from country *i* to country *j* in year *t*. RTA = reciprocal trade agreement. MA = mutual-agreement index. AA = Asymmetric-agreement index. All regressions are estimated using 5-year panel from 1975 to 2005 and include exporter-by-time, importer-by-time, and exporter-to-importer bilateral fixed effects omitted in the table for brevity. Robust standard errors are in parentheses. ** denotes the null hypothesis is rejected at the 0.01 level.

Source: USDA, Economic Research Service.

Table 5 and 6 show the parameter estimates from our RTA phase-in gravity models for total agricultural trade. We calculate the sum of the contemporaneous and lag coefficients of *MA* and *AA* occurring over 10 years to gauge the cumulative impact of RTAs on partner trade as these agreements mature. The percentage change in trade expansion and trade contraction are reported as "total *MA* effect" and "total *AA* effect" when the sum of the parameter estimates $MA_t + {}_{MAt\text{-}5} + {}_{MAt\text{-}10}$ and $AA_t + {}_{AAt\text{-}5} + {}_{AAt\text{-}10}$ were determined to be significantly different from zero via Wald test statistics, respectively.

Table 5. Agricultural trade expansion derived from generalized gravity equations with RTA phase-in effects'

	1	2	3	4	5	6	7	8	9
	ALL imports from ALL	HIC imports from ALL	ALL imports from HIC	HIC imports from HIC	LIC imports from HIC	LIC imports from ALL	ALL imports from LIC	LIC imports from LIC	HIC imports from LIC
MAijt	0.18**	0.07	0.03	0.17*	-0.06	0.28**	0.35**	0.63**	0.08
	(0.05)	(0.07)	(0.07)	(0.07)	(0.14)	(0.10)	(0.10)	(0.17)	(0.15)
MAijt-5	0.24**	0.23**	0.21**	0.32**	0.03	0.19	0.07	0.02	-0.10
	(0.06)	(0.07)	(0.07)	(0.07)	(0.20)	(0.13)	(0.13)	(0.21)	(0.21)
MAijt-10	0.29**	0.14	0.10	0.05	-0.21	0.13	0.21	0.26	-0.04
	(0.07)	(0.07)	(0.07)	(0.06)	(0.22)	(0.15)	(0.17)	(0.22)	(0.33)
Constant	13.85**	15.49**	16.12**	17.86**	14.44**	13.18**	12.99**	12.86**	14.46**
	(0.22)	(0.07)	(0.20)	(0.30)	(0.05)	(0.39)	(0.36)	(0.15)	(0.15)
MAijt sum	0.72**	0.44**	0.34**	0.53**	-0.24	0.61**	0.63**	0.90**	-0.06
	(0.08)	(0.09)	(0.09)	(0.09)	(0.29)	(0.17)	(0.17)	(0.23)	(0.40)
Total MA effect	1.05	0.55	0.40	0.70		0.84	0.88	1.46	
Adjusted R^2	0.86	0.90	0.90	0.94	0.85	0.81	0.82	0.76	0.86
F-statistic	14.51	16.59	19.35	31.69	11.04	9.44	7.67	5.95	7.36
Root MSE	1.18	0.94	0.91	0.54	1.05	1.32	1.35	1.53	1.10
No. of observations	19,225	8,076	8,263	2,994	5,269	11,149	10,962	5,880	5,082

Notes: The dependent variable is the natural log of agricultural bilateral trade (lnXijt) from country *i* to country *j* in year *t*. RTA = reciprocal trade agreement. MA = mutual-agreement index. AA = asymmetric-agreement index. HIC = high-income countries. LIC = low-income countries. ALL = both high-income and low-income countries. All regressions are estimated using 5-year panel data from 1975 to 2005 and include exporter-by-time, importer-by-time, and exporter-to-importer bilateral fixed effects omitted in the table for brevity. The "total MA effect" measures the percentage change in bilateral trade attributable to mutual membership in an RTA. It is calculated when the MAijt sum is significantly different than zero. Standard errors are in parentheses. They are calculated using White's heteroskedastic robust standard errors. * and ** denote the null hypothesis is rejected at the 0.05 and 0.01 level, respectively.

Source: USDA, Economic Research Service.

To examine whether RTAs may have had an impact on various partner combinations, we divided our global sample of observed trade flows into high-income (HIC), low-income (LIC), and all (ALL) exporter/importer groupings. We then ran the dummy-intensive gravity model on the following eight subsamples: ALL imports from ALL, HIC imports from ALL, ALL imports from HIC, HIC imports from HIC, LIC imports from HIC, LIC imports from

ALL, ALL imports from LIC, LIC imports from LIC, and HIC imports from LIC.

The sum of the generated *MA* parameter estimates from our global sample of 19,225 agricultural trade flows equals 0.72 (table 5, column 1). This sum is similar to the 10-year cumulative MA estimates of 0.76 and 0.81, denoting trade expansion for total merchandise trade estimated by Baier and Bergstrand (2007) and for agricultural trade calculated by Grant and Lambert (2008), respectively.[23] Our estimate indicates that the longrun cumulative impact of mutual membership in RTAs increases bilateral agricultural trade 105 percent, on average, beyond what would have occurred in the absence of these agreements when allowing for 10 years of phase-in effects.

Inspection of the empirical results from the various subsamples reveals that much of the agricultural trade expansion identified in the global sample stemmed from mutual RTA membership between countries in the low-income grouping. The payoff to agricultural LIC exporters belonging to the same RTA as their LIC partner was particularly pronounced, increasing 1.5-fold, on average (table 5, column 8). This finding suggests that RTAs may be a particularly effective policy instrument, serving as a catalyst to more open agricultural markets in the developing world.

Interestingly, there was no discernable increase in bilateral agricultural trade at mean values due to mutual RTA membership by either HIC exporters supplying affiliate LIC markets or by LIC exporters supplying affiliate HIC markets (columns 5 and 9). However, trade increased, on average, for HIC agricultural exporters supplying HIC markets when partners were members of the same RTA (column 4). This trade increase is 70 percent in the long run.

The rise in RTA-member agricultural exports to RTA-member partners came at the expense of trade with other agricultural suppliers. In the global sample, agricultural sales fell 49 percent, on average, for exporters supplying import partners affiliated with RTAs to which the exporters did not belong (table 6, column 1). When comparing subsample results (columns 2-9), agricultural trade contraction was the least, falling 24 percent in the long run, for an HIC supplier exporting to a country in the set of ALL importers (column 3).[24]

Table 6. Agricultural trade contraction derived from generalized gravity equations with RTA phase-in effects

	1	2	3	4	5	6	7	8	9
	ALL imports from ALL	HIC imports from ALL	ALL imports from HIC	HIC imports from HIC	LIC imports from HIC	LIC imports from ALL	ALL imports from LIC	LIC imports from LIC	HIC imports from LIC
	-0.15**	-0.04	0.02	-0.16*	0.19	-0.23*	-0.30**	-0.59**	0.03
AAijt	(0.05)	(0.07)	(0.07)	(0.08)	(0.15)	(0.10)	(0.10)	(0.17)	(0.15)
	-0.26**	-0.24**	-0.27**	-0.35**	-0.14	-0.23	-0.06	-0.03	0.09
AAijt-5	(0.06)	(0.08)	(0.07)	(0.07)	(0.20)	(0.13)	(0.13)	(0.21)	(0.21)
	-0.26**	-0.14	-0.04	-0.03	0.45*	-0.04	-0.23	-0.23	-0.05
AAijt-10	(0.07)	(0.08)	(0.07)	(0.07)	(0.22)	(0.15)	(0.16)	(0.21)	(0.31)
	14.79**	16.46**	15.51**	18.26**	13.90**	13.59**	13.78**	13.60**	14.52**
Constant	(0.18)	(0.10)	(0.30)	(0.36)	(0.26)	(0.31)	(0.29)	(0.30)	(0.36)
AAijt sum	-0.67** (0.08)	-0.42** (0.09)	-0.28** (0.10)	-0.54** (0.09)	0.50 (0.27)	-0.50** (0.16)	-0.58** (0.17)	-0.85** (0.23)	0.07 (0.35)
Total AA effect	-0.49	-0.34	-0.24	-0.42		-0.39	-0.44	-0.57	
Adjusted R^2	0.86	0.90	0.90	0.94	0.85	0.81	0.82	0.76	0.86
F-statistic	14.46	16.54	19.35	32.02	11.10	9.43	7.66	5.95	7.34
Root MSE	1.18	0.94	0.91	0.54	1.05	1.32	1.35	1.53	1.10
No. of observations	19,225	8,076	8,263	2,994	5,269	11,149	10,962	5,880	5,082

Notes: The dependent variable is the natural log of agricultural bilateral trade (lnXijt) from country *i* to country *j* in year *t*. RTA = reciprocal trade agreement. MA = mutual-agreement index. AA = asymmetric-agreement index. HIC = high-income countries. LIC = low-income countries. ALL = both high-income and low-income countries. All regressions are estimated using 5-year panel data from 1975 to 2005 and include exporter-by-time, importer-by-time, and exporter-to-importer bilateral fixed effects omitted in the table for brevity. The "total AA effect" measures the percentage change in bilateral trade attributable to mutual membership in an RTA. It is calculated when the AAijt sum is significantly different than zero. Standard errors are in parentheses. They are calculated using White's heteroskedastic robust standard errors. * and ** denote the null hypothesis is rejected at the 0.05 and 0.01 level, respectively.

Source: USDA, Economic Research Service.

Model Tradeoffs

RTAs are viewed by some analysts as a vehicle for government policymakers to use to circumvent domestic regulations in foreign countries by virtue of their ability to get "behind the border" and remove domestic barriers in foreign countries that inhibit partner trade. Lawrence (1996) posits, for instance, a link between the formation of RTAs and antitrust rules, product standards, corporate governance, tax codes, and internal shipping regulations. Yet such phenomena are not included in gravity equations because they are difficult, if not impossible, to quantify.

The absence of factors driving trade, such as domestic rules and regulations, in our benchmark and sample-selection models may yield biased and inconsistent coefficient estimates attributable to omitted variables. Errorsin-variable bias arises when variables omitted in applied models are correlated with both the dependent variable and one or more of the explanatory variables.

The first generalized model we estimate includes year, exporter-by-time, importer-by-time, and exporter-to-importer fixed effects. Year dummies control for numerous factors, including inflation common to all countries and the general increase in trade taking place due to globalization. The countryby-time fixed effects pick up domestic policies and country-specific macroeconomic shocks characterizing exporters and importers, as well as what Anderson and van Wincoop (2004) refer to as "multilateral resistances" that affect each trading partner. The exporter-to-importer fixed effects control for unobserved heterogeneity, such as unique institutional linkages and political arrangements characterizing each country pair.

The empirical results show that gravity models that do not comprehensively account for heterogeneity, via the inclusion of appropriate fixed effects, produce upwardly biased RTA coefficients. Note, for example, parameter estimates for the statistically significant RTA variables denoting MA and AA generated from the contemporaneous generalized gravity model are substantially smaller (less than one-half) than corresponding coefficients in either of the two conventional models.

The second generalized model we estimate is similar to the first. It includes the same set of fixed effects but also accounts for RTA lag effects. Empirical results indicate that the trade impacts of RTAs grow as producers and consumers adjust to policy-induced changes in the structure of markets and as the implementing provisions of these agreements are phased in over a period of 10 years.

The shortcoming of the two generalized models is that the intensive use of fixed effects sweeps away specific variables that trade theory identifies as driving cross-border trade. Neither of the generalized models, for example, can accommodate the relative resource endowment variable. Thus, no tests can be performed to determine if the exporter/importer-to-land/labor ratio is statistically significant. By contrast, both our benchmark and sample-selection models provide empirical evidence that relative factor endowment is an important driver of trade in agriculture, just as theory suggests.

Finally, we address concerns expressed in the literature about the possibility of bias in parameter estimates obtained from log-linear gravity models. The dependent variable in log-linear models is not really bilateral trade, but bilateral trade contingent on a trading relationship because the log of zero is not defined. Our empirical results show that dropping missing and/or unreported trade, as is commonly done, generates modestly biased estimates for some independent variables, including that of MA and AA. Interestingly, the coefficients generated by the OLS models were virtually identical and of the same level of statistical significance as those derived from the MLE models for the other explanatory variables (e.g., relative factor endowments).

SUMMARY OF RESULTS

In this study, ERS examined the impact of reciprocal trade agreements on bilateral trade expansion and trade contraction in the world agricultural marketplace. We used a generic dummy variable to identify the influence on partner trade of mutual RTA membership. We innovated by developing and deploying a similarly constructed dummy variable, but one that is capable of detecting the influence of these agreements on trade between RTA member countries and their nonmember partners.

Four types of gravity equations were estimated: a benchmark model, a Heckman sample-selection model, a generalized model focused on contemporaneous impacts, and a generalized model that accommodates RTA phase-in effects. Model results provide empirical evidence that RTAs augment trade among and between countries mutually belonging to a common RTA, on average. We also find evidence that this increase in trade comes at the expense of other suppliers. Imports of agricultural goods by countries that belong to RTAs typically fall from exporters who do not share a common RTA membership with their trading partner. Interestingly, results in each of the four types of models show that the percentage increase in bilateral trade attributable to mutual RTA membership is greater than the percentage decrease in partner trade due to asymmetric membership.

Results from the benchmark models indicate that joint RTA membership, on average, boosts agricultural trade 93 percent in the long run, while the decrease in bilateral trade due to asymmetric membership is 46 percent. The Heckman sample-selection models depict somewhat lower longrun RTA impacts on bilateral trade. These models, which, unlike the OLS models, account for the absence of partner trade, show that membership in a common RTA generates 84 percent more agricultural trade between partner countries. Results also show that exports by countries supplying agricultural products to importers belonging to RTAs to which the exporter is not a member fall by 43 percent.

Our first generalized model focuses exclusively on the contemporaneous effect of RTAs. It generates much smaller RTA impacts than either the benchmark or Heckman models. This is due to the generalized model's comprehensive control of both observed and unobserved heterogeneity. Empirical results from this generalized model show that mutual RTA membership increases bilateral trade by 34 percent in the long run, on average. The model also shows that asymmetric membership decreases agricultural trade by 26 percent for countries importing from export suppliers not affiliated with an RTA to which the importer is a member.

Our second generalized model accounts not only for the contemporaneous impact of RTAs but also for their lagged effects. In our view, this model generates the most accurate estimates of RTA-induced trade expansion and trade contraction. It allows for implementation of the free-trade provisions of RTAs to be phased in over a period of years. It also allows for the time often required for market participants to adjust their behavior to RTA-induced changes in market structure.

The generalized model with phase-in effects estimates the 10-year cumulative increase in agricultural exports to RTA partners to be 105 percent in the long run (on average), or triple the contemporaneous impact. The cumulative decrease in trade for an exporter supplying agricultural goods to an import partner affiliated with an RTA to which the exporter does not belong is estimated to be 49 percent, almost double the contemporaneous impact of 26 percent. These findings demonstrate that the trade impacts of RTAs grow as producers and consumers adjust to policy-induced changes in the structure of markets.

Subsample estimations using the generalized gravity model with RTA phase-in effects revealed that much of the agricultural trade expansion identified in the global sample stemmed from mutual RTA membership between countries in the low-income grouping. The payoff was particularly pronounced when both partners were members of the same RTA, increasing 1.5-fold over the long run. This finding suggests that even though many policies in low-income countries continue to protect agriculture, RTAs are relatively effective instruments in removing impediments to bilateral trade. It also indicates that RTAs may open markets that were previously closed or nearly closed within the developing world. Even a small increase in agricultural trade induced by the formation of an RTA between two low-income countries generates a large percentage change in trade when the previous level of trade between them was low.

Interestingly, there was no discernable increase in agricultural trade due to mutual RTA membership by either high-income country exporters supplying affiliate low-income country markets or by low-income country exporters supplying affiliate high-income country markets, on average. Many developing countries, nevertheless, place a high priority on forging trade agreements with high-income countries rather than with low-income countries.

Policymakers may wish to think strategically when selecting partner countries with whom to form trade agreements. For example, a country is less likely to experience the adverse effects of import trade diversion when it chooses to form a trade alliance with countries whose exports are cost competitive with other foreign sources of supply. Similarly, a country is more likely to gain from export expansion by forging agreements with countries having high tariffs. The volume of cross-border trade is surely to grow with such countries as import levies are negotiated downward.

REFERENCES

Aitken, Norman D. 1973. "The Effect of the EEC and EFTA on European Trade: A Temporal Cross-Section Analysis. *American Economic Review,* Vol. 63: 881-891.

Anderson, James E., and Eric van Wincoop. 2004. "Trade Costs." *Journal of Economic Literature,* Vol. XLII: 691-751, September.

____. 2003. "Gravity with Gravitas: A Solution to the Border Puzzle." *American Economic Review,* Vol. 93: 170-192, March.

Armington, Paul S. 1969. "A Theory of Demand for Products Distinguished by Place of Production." *IMF Staff Papers*, Vol. 16: 159-176.

Baier, Scott L, Jeffrey H. Bergstrand, Peter Egger, and Patrick A. McLaughlin. 2008. "Do Economic Integration Agreements Actually Work? Issues in Understanding the Causes and Consequences of Growth of Regionalism." *The World Economy,* pp. 461-497.

Baier, Scott L. and Jeffrey H. Bergstrand. 2007. "Do Free Trade Agreements Actually Increase Members' International Trade?" *Journal of International Economics,* Vol. 71: 72-95.

Baldwin, R. 2006. "The Euro's Trade Effects." Working Paper No. 594. ECB Workshop: What Effect Is EMU Having on the Euro Area and Its Member Countries?" March, www.ecb.int/pub/pdf/scpwps/ecbwp594.pdf.

Bayoumi, Tamim, and Barry Eichengreen. 1997. "Is Regionalism Simply a Diversion? Evidence From the Evolution of the EC and EFTA." In *Regionalism versus Multilateral Trade Arrangements*. Takatoshi Ito and Anne O. Krueger (eds.), pp. 141-164. Chicago: The University of Chicago Press.

Bergsten, C. Fred. 1998. "Open Regionalism." In *Globalization of the World Economy*, Vol. 4, Northampton, MA.: Elgar.

___. 1996. "Competitive Liberalization and Global Free Trade: A Vision for the Early 21st Century," Working Paper No. 96-15. Washington, DC: Institute for International Economics.

Bhagwati, Jagdish, and Arvind Panagariya. 1996. "The Theory of Preferential Trade Agreements: Historical Evolution and Current Trends." *The American Economic Review*, Vol. 86: 82-87, May.

Centre d'Etudes Prospectives et d'Informations Internationales, 2005. Database: CEPI, www.cepii.org/anglaisgraph/bdd/distances.htm.

Cheng, I-Hui, and Howard J. Wall. 2005. "Controlling for Heterogeneity in Gravity Models of Trade and Integration." *Federal Reserve Bank of St. Louis Review*, Vol. 87(1): 49-63, January/February, research.stlouisfed.org/publications/review/05/01/Cheng.pdf.

Clarete, Ramon, Christopher Edmonds, and Jessica Seddon Wallack. 2003. "Asian Regionalism and Its Effects on Trade in the 1980s and 1990s." *Journal of Asian Economics,* Vol. 14: 91-129.

Deardorff, Alan V. 1998. "Determinants of Bilateral Trade: Does Gravity Work in a Neoclassical World?" In *The Regionalization of the World Economy,* J.A. Frankel (ed.), pp. 7-22. Chicago: University of Chicago Press.

Dixit, Avinash K., and Joseph E. Siglitz. 1977. "Monopolistic Competition and Optimum Product Diversity." *American Economic Review,* Vol. 67(3): 297-308, June.

Eaton, Jonathan, and Samuel Kortum. 2002. "Technology, Geography, and Trade." *Econometrica,* Vol. 70: 1741-1779, September.

Eichengreen, Barry, and Douglas A. Irwin. 1995. "Trade Blocs, Currency Blocs and the Reorientation of World Trade in the 1930s." *Journal of International Economics,* Vol. 38: 1-24.

Eicher, Theo S., and Christian Henn. 2009. "In Search of WTO Trade Effects: Preferential Trade Agreements Promote Trade Strongly, But Unevenly."

IMF Working Paper No. 09/31, February, econpapers.repec. org/paper/imfimfwpa/09_2f31.htm.

Egger, Peter, and Michael Pfaffermayr. 2003. "The Proper Panel Econometric Specification of the Gravity Equation: A Three-Way Model With Bilateral Interaction Effects. *Empirical Economics,* Vol. 28: 571-580.

Egger, Peter. 2000. "A Note on the Proper Econometric Specification of the Gravity Equation." *Economic Letters,* Vol. 66: 25-31.

Endoh, M. 1999. "Trade Creation and Trade Diversion in the EEC, the LAFTA and the CMEA: 1960-1994." *Applied Economics,* Vol. 31: 207-216.

Evenett, Simon J., and Wolfgang Keller. 2002. "On Theories Explaining the Success of the Gravity Equation." *Journal of Political Economy,* Vol. 110: 281-316.

Feenstra, Robert C. 2003. *Advanced International Trade: Theory and Evidence.* Princeton, NJ: Princeton University Press.

Feenstra, Robert C. 2002. "Border Effects and the Gravity Equation: Consistent Methods of Estimation." *Scottish Journal of Political Economy,* Vol. 49: 491-506, November.

Feenstra, Robert C., James R. Markusen, and Andrew K. Rose. 2001. "Using the Gravity Equation to Differentiate Among Alternative Theories of Trade." *Canadian Journal of Economics,* Vol. 34: 430-447, May.

Fiorentino, Roberto V., Luis Verdeja, and Christelle Toqueboeuf. 2006. "The Changing Landscape of Regional Trade Agreements: 2006 Update." Discussion Paper No. 8. World Trade Organization, www.wto.org/english/ res_e/booksp_e/discussion_papers12a_e.pdf.

Ghosh, S., and S. Yamarik. 2004. "Are Regional Trading Arrangements Trade Creating?: An Application of Extreme Bounds Analysis." *Journal of International Economics,* Vol. 63: 369-395.

Grant, Jason H., and Dayton M. Lambert. 2008a. "Do Regional Trade Agreements Increase Members' Agricultural Trade?" *American Journal of Agricultural Economics,* Vol. 90: 765-782, August.

___. 2008b. "Has the World Trade Organization Promoted Successful Regional Trade Agreements?" Paper presented at Annual Meeting of the American Agricultural Economics Association, Orlando, FL, July 27-29.

___. 2005. "Regionalism in World Agricultural Trade: Lessons from Gravity Model Estimation." Paper presented at Annual Meeting of the Agricultural Economics Association, Providence, RI, July 24-27.

Heckman, James J., 1979. "Sample Selection Bias as a Specification Error." *Econometrica,* Vol. 47: 153-161.

Koo, Won W., P. Lynn Kennedy, and Anatoliy Skripnitchenko. 2006. "Regional Preferential Trade Agreements: Trade Creation and Diversion Effects. *Review of Agricultural Economics,* Vol. 28(3): 408-415.

Lambert, David, and Shahera McKoy. 2009. "Trade Creation and Diversion Effects of Preferential Trade Associations on Agricultural and Food Trade." *Journal of Agricultural Economics*, Vol. 60(1): 17-39.

Lawrence, Robert Z. 1996, *Regionalism, Multilateralism, and Deeper Integration*. The Brookings Institution: Washington, DC, 1996.

Linders, Gert-Jan, and Henri L.F. De Groot. 2006. "Estimation of the Gravity Equation in the Presence of Zero Flows." Working Paper No. 06-072/3. Amsterdam: Tinbergen Institute, August.

Magee, Christopher S.P. 2008. "New Measures of Trade Creation and Trade Diversion." *Journal of International Economics,* Vol. 75: 349-362.

Martin, Will, and Cong S. Pham. 2008. "Estimating the Gravity Model When Zero Trade Flows Are Frequent." Development Economic Research Group: World Bank, February, wmartinweb.googlepages.com/gravity feb_08.pdf .

Mátyás, Lászl6. 1997. "Proper Econometric Specification of the Gravity Model." *The World Economy,* Vol. 20: 432-434.

Meade, J.E. 1956. *The Theory of Customs Unions.* Amsterdam: North-Holland Publishing.

Oh, Chang Hoon. 2006. "Technical Appendix on the Regional Economic Integration Database." In *Regional Economic Integration.* Michele Fratianni (ed.), pp 261-277. Elsevier: New York.

Palgrave. 1987. *The New Palgrave: A Dictionary of Economics*. John Eatwell, Murray Milgate, and Peter Newman (eds.). London: The MacMillan Press Limited.

Pöyhonen, P. 1963. "A Tentative Model for the Volume of Trade Between Countries." *Weltwirtschaftliches Archiv,* Vol. 90: 93-99.

Rose, Andrew K. 2006. Database, faculty.haas.berkeley.edu/arose/RecRes. htm#Software.

___. 2004 "Do We Really Know That the WTO Increases Trade?" *The American Economic Review,* Vol. 94: 98-114, March.

Rose, Andrew K., and Eric van Wincoop. 2001. "National Money as a Barrier to International Trade: The Real Case for Currency Union. *The American Economic Review,* Vol. 91: 386-390, May.

Sandberg, H. Mikael, James L. Seale, Jr., and Timothy G. Taylor. 2006. "History, Regionalism, and CARICOM Trade: A Gravity Model Analysis." *Journal of Development Studies,* Vol. 42(5): 795-811, July.

Sapir, A. 2001. "Domino Effects in Western European Regional Trade, 1960-1992." *European Journal of Political Economy,* Vol. 17: 377-388.

Silva, J.M.C. Santos, and Silvana Tenreyro. 2006. "The Log of Gravity." *The Review of Economics and Statistics,* Vol. 88: 641-658, November.

Soloaga, Isidro, and L. Alan Winters. 2001. "Regionalism in the Nineties: What Effect on Trade?" *North American Journal of Economics and Finance,* Vol. 12: 1-29.

Subramanian, Arvind, and Shang-Jin Wei. 2007. "The WTO Promotes Trade, Strongly But Unevenly." *Journal of International Economics,* Vol. 72: 151-175, May.

Tang, Donny. 2005. "Effects of the Regional Trading Arrangements on Trade: Evidence from the NAFTA, ANZCER, and ASEAN Countries, 1989-2000." *Journal of International Trade and Economic Development,* Vol. 14(2): 241-265.

Tinbergen, J. 1962. *Shaping the World Economy.* New York: Twentieth Century Fund.

Tomz, M., J.L. Goldstein, and D. Rivers. 2007. "Do We Really Know That the WTO Increases Trade? Comment." *American Economic Review,* Vol. 97(5): 2005-2018.

UN Statistical Office. 2008. Database: UN Comtrade, unstats.un.org/unsd/comtrade/mr/rfReportersList.aspx.

United Nations Food and Agricultural Organization. 2008. FAOSTAT, faostat.fao.org/faostat/collections?subset=agriculture

U.S. Department of Agriculture, Agricultural Research Service. 2005. "Surface Distance Between Two Points of Latitude and Longitude," www.wcrl.ars.usda.gov/cec/java/lat-long.htm.

Viner, Jacob. 1950. *The Customs Union Issue.* New York: Carnegie Endowment for International Peace.

Vicard, Vincent. 2009. "On Trade Creation and Regional Trade Agreements: Does Depth Matter?" *Review of World Economics,* Vol. 145(2): 167-187, July.

Vollrath, Thomas, Mark Gehlhar, and Charles Hallahan. 2009. "Bilateral Import Protection, Free Trade Agreements, and Other Factors Influencing Trade Flows in Agriculture and Clothing." *Journal of Agricultural Economics,* Vol. 60.2: 298-317, June.

Vollrath, Thomas, Charles Hallahan, and Mark Gehlhar. 2006. "Consumer Demand and Cost Factors Shape the Global Trade Network in Commodity and Manufactured Foods." *Canadian Journal of Agricultural Economics,*

Vol. 54: 497-512, December, www3.interscience.wiley.com/cgi-bin/fulltext/118594018/PDFSTART.

Wainio, John. 2006. "The U.S. Perspective on Bilateral and Regional Trade Agreements." Paper presented at ABARE Outlook Conference, Canberra, Australia, March 1.

Washington Post. 2009. "Trade Backsliding: Small Signs of Protectionism Are Popping Up Around the Globe," April 23.

Wei, Shang-Jin, and Jeffrey A. Frankel. 1997. "Open Versus Closed Trade Blocs." In *Regionalism Versus Multilateral Trade Arrangements*. Takatoshi Ito and Anne O. Krueger (eds.), pp. 119-140. Chicago: The University of Chicago Press.

Westerlund, Joakim, and Fredrik Wilhelmsson. 2006. "Estimating the Gravity Model Without Gravity Using Panel Data." February, www.nek.lu.se/nekfwi/Estimating%20the%20gravity%20model.pdf.

World Bank. 2005. *World Development Indicators, 2005,* www.worldbank.org/data/wdi2005/index.html.

World Trade Organization. 2010. "Regional Trade Agreements," www.wto.org/english/tratop_e/region_e/region_e.htm/

Zahniser, Steven S., Daniel Pick, Greg Pompelli, and Mark J. Gehlhar. 2004. "Trade Liberalization in the Western Hemisphere: Impacts on U.S. Agricultural Exports." In *U.S. Agriculture and the Free Trade Area of the Americas*. Mary E. Burfisher (ed.). Agricultural Economics Report No. 827, U.S. Department of Agriculture, Economic Research Service. March, www.ers.usda.gov/publications/aer827/

APPENDIX: ECONOMIC TRADE THEORY AND ADVANCES IN APPLIED ANALYSES

In the abstract world of neoclassical economics, relative price differentials provide incentives for cross-border trade that result in price convergence. However, given trade impediments such as transportation and other transaction costs in the real world, trade and domestic price differentials can persist if transaction costs equal differences in production costs. To further empirical understanding about the forces underpinning bilateral trade flows, Tinbergen (1962) and Pöyhonen (1963) pioneered estimation of gravity equations. The basic model can be expressed as follows:

$$Vij = f(Y_i, Y_j, D_{ij}) \tag{1}$$

where V_{ij}, the value of trade between countries *i* and *j*, is a positive function of Y_i and Y_j, the income (i.e., market size) of *i* and *j*, and a negative function of D_{ij}, the distance separating the two trading partners signifying transaction costs of commercial activity.

Many variations of the basic gravity model have been used in the literature to examine the factors hypothesized to drive product specialization and trade. Modified equations often include variables denoting specific supply conditions at the origin (e.g., factor endowments, technology), additional demand conditions at the destination (e.g., per capita income), and/or numerous economic forces that either assist or resist the movement of bilateral trade (e.g., colonial linkages, trade agreements).

Applied gravity analyses fell out of favor for a number of years due to data and statistical problems as well as to concerns about the absence of clear linkages to economic trade theory. Recent contributions in the theoretical and applied literature have, however, enhanced credibility and sparked a revival in gravity-based research.

A number of studies have strengthened microeconomic foundations. Deardorff (1998) addresses whether gravity models can work in the neoclassical world. He shows that the gravity equations are able to accommodate both the perfectly competitive Heckscher-Ohlin model and the monopolistic-competitive model of Dixit-Stiglitz (1977). Feenstra et al. (2001) develop a national (Armington) product and a monopolistic competition model, both of which include transaction costs. They conclude that a wider range of theories than previously recognized is consistent with the gravity-type equation. Evenett and Keller (2002) demonstrate that the gravity framework can be used to test for increasing-returns-to-scale and relative-factor-endowment explanations of trade under conditions of perfect and imperfect specialization. Eaton and Kortum (2002) derive a gravity model from the Ricardian theory of international trade. A recent contribution to this literature is the work of Anderson and van Wincoop (2003, 2004). They developed an analytical framework that establishes linkages between trade theory, in which p rices play a central equilibrating role, and the generalized gravity model.

Anderson and van Wincoop (AvW) manipulate the constant-elasticity-of-substitution (CES) expenditure system to derive an operational model based upon trade costs. Market-clearing conditions are imposed to solve for general-equilibrium prices, prices that embody bilateral resistances confronting both the exporter and the importer with all of their trading partners. The most important insight obtained from their gravity model is that bilateral trade depends not only on the bilateral drivers, such as distance, characterizing the joint partnership of *i* and *j*, but also on multilateral drivers confronting exporter *i* and importer *j* in their other markets.

The generalized gravity equation that emerges from AvW's framework is consistent with economic theory:

$$\ln(X_{ij}) = \ln(Y_i) + \ln(Y_j) - \ln(Y_w) + (1-\sigma)\left[\ln(TI_{ij}) - \ln(P_i) - \ln(P_j)\right] \quad (2)$$

where X_{ij} is the value of exports from *i* to *j*; Y_i, Y_j, and Y_w are the outputs of country *i*, *j*, and the world (*w*), respectively; a is the elasticity of substitution between the countries' goods; TI_{ij} represents trade impediments; P_i captures "outward multilateral resistances" that depict the average trade resistance between origin *i* and its importing partner; P_j embodies "inward multilateral resistances" that represent destination *j*'s average trade resistance with its supplying partners; and the *O*s denote income shares.

Fixed-effects statistical models can account for unobservable omitted variables (Feenstra, 2003). Given that the fixed-effects models are computationally easier to estimate than customized nonlinear least squares (NLS) models, most applied researchers have adopted the least squares dummy variables (LSDV) approach to estimating generalized gravity equations. The prototype model of the LSDV-type is as follows:[25]

$$\ln(X_{ij}) = \gamma_i + \gamma_j + \alpha_1 \ln(Y_i) + \alpha_2 \ln(Y_j) + \sum_{m=1}^{M} \beta_m \ln(TI_{ij}^m) + \varepsilon_{ij} \quad (3)$$

where the fixed effects (γ_i) and (γ_j) control for multilateral prices, each $TIij^m$ represents a proxy vector denoting bilateral trade costs and ε_{ij} refers to the disturbance term.[26]

Recent developments in the applied literature have advanced gravity analyses by addressing statistical issues that had led to model misspecification and incorrect interpretation of empirical results in the early years. Mátyás (1997) and Egger and Pfaffermayr (2003) have shown that proper use of fixed effects can correct for omitted variables. Mátyás maintains that gravity models that test the significance of trading blocs are misspecified unless they are specified as a triple-index model that accounts for exporter, importer, and time fixed effects. Egger and Pfaffermayr assert that proper specification of the gravity equation includes, in addition to Mátyás's three indexes, bilateral fixed effects. Baier and Bergstrand (2007) present a case for using countryby-time and country-pair fixed effects in a theoretically motivated gravity equation. Baldwin (2006) recommends ignoring gravity results that do not comprehensively control for such heterogeneity.

End Notes

[1] According to the WTO's Committee on Regional Trade Agreements (CRTA), as of July 31, 2010, there are a total of 474 bilateral/regional trade agreements in force (World Trade Organization, 2010).

[2] One reviewer expressed skepticism that any useful information could be generated from highly aggregate gravity models. Our view is that applied research is needed across numerous levels of aggregation if economists are to provide information about economic relationships that can be helpful to policymakers and can help educate the public. It is important to be able to generalize about the effect of policy instruments, such as bilateral/regional trade agreements, on the patterns of world trade and economic welfare. It is also important to gain insight about the impact of such policy instruments on individual sectors, commodities, periods, and specific agreements. Additional research is needed that focuses attention on the impacts of specific agreements on trade in agriculture, both at the sector level and across individual commodities and also on the impacts of RTAs on exports (imports) of individual countries.

[3] The trade-diversion variables used in the Tang and Magee studies equal one when *either* country *i* or *j* belongs to an RTA. These dummies depart from Viner's concept of trade diversion in that Viner restricted attention to imports by an RTA member country from a nonmember supplier.

[4] Other studies that have used generic RTA indexes in a panel setting include Rose (2006), Tomz et al. (2007), Subramanian and Wei (2007), Baier and Bergstrand (2007), and Grant and Lambert (2008a). But these indexes have been restricted to portray trade creation, not trade diversion.

[5] A reviewer asked why we never tried random-effects estimation. We did not use this approach, as others have rejected it for theoretical and empirical reasons. Baier et al. (2008) reject using the random-effects model in gravity analyses on conceptual grounds. They point out that unobserved time-invariant variables influence both the presence of RTAs as well as the volume of trade. In the fixed-effects model, these unobservable variables are controlled by using country-pair fixed effects. The problem with the random-effects model is that it assumes zero correlation between these bilateral fixed effects and RTAs. Moreover, Egger (2000) tested for fixed versus random effects after estimating gravity equations with panel data. Using the Hausman test, he found overwhelming empirical evidence for the rejection of random-effects gravity model relative to a fixed-effects model.

[6] A reviewer expressed concern that the GDP variables in our model may induce endogeneity. Baier and Bergstrand (2007) addressed this issue, as well as other possible sources of endogeneity, in gravity equations. They contend that while GDP is a function of total exports and total imports, the inclusion of country *i*'s income and country *j*'s income as independent variables in gravity equations is not a likely cause of endogeneity because each importer has many suppliers and each exporter sends its goods to many destination markets.

[7] The 9-percent threshold serves to denote the level at which the ability to communicate is viewed as not imposing substantial transaction costs.

[8] Rose identifies four types of dummy variables that can be used to control for colonial heritage in gravity models: (1) a binary variable which is unity if *i* and *j* were ever colonies after 1945 with the same colonizer, (2) a binary variable which is unity if *i* is a colony of *j* at time *t* or vice versa, (3) a binary variable which is unity if *i* ever colonized *j* or vice versa, and (4) a binary variable is unity if *i* and *j* remained part of the same nation during the sample. We arbitrarily chose the first type of binary variable to depict colonial heritage in our models.

[9] The $\gamma_t = 1$ when year is equal to *t* and 0 otherwise, where $t = 1975, 1980, \ldots 2005$.

[10] The two RTA dummies were constructed using "full-year" enforcement, with full year referring to at least 8 months of agreement implementation.

[11] Linders and de Groot (2006) investigated other methods for dealing with zero-trade flows, including various extensions of Tobit estimation, truncated regression, probit regression, and replacement of zero flows with arbitrary numbers. They found the sample-selection model econometrically preferable to these alternative approaches.

[12] OLS parameter estimates are likely to be downwardly biased and inconsistent should incidental truncation arise ($p \neq 0$). In such situations, the OLS regression is misspecified as it excludes the Inverse Mills Ratio as an independent variable. As a result, OLS coefficients are attenuated (i.e., biased toward zero) and the error variance (σ^2_U) is underestimated.

[13] To circumvent a possible identification problem, we followed common practice by excluding an exogenous variable in the outcome equation that is included in the selection equation. One reviewer was critical of our choice of dropping the language-similarity variable. However, William Greene of New York University informed us (in personal communication) that the identification restriction was not only a "nonissue" when using the MLE, but that, if a restriction was imposed, it made little difference which variable was chosen to exclude from the selection equation. Moreover, we did not estimate the Heckman model in two stages, but rather simultaneously, using maximum likelihood estimator.

[14] $\gamma_{it} = 1$ for exporter *i* in year *t* and 0 otherwise, $\gamma_{it} = 1$ for importer *j* in year *t* and 0 otherwise, and $\gamma_{it} = 1$ for country *i* exporting to importer *j* and 0 otherwise (where $i = 1, 2, \ldots 69$, $j = 1, 2, \ldots 69$, and $t = 1975, 1980 \ldots 2005$). A reviewer asked why γ_{it} did not pick up the effects of RTAs. The answer is that the TP indices, unlike the country-pair fixed effects, are not invariant over the 31-year time period of the analysis. MA and AA are coded dynamically to account for the changing composition of RTAs through time as countries join/ depart from the specific agreements.

[15] The 69 countries include Algeria, Argentina, Australia, Austria, Bangladesh, Belgium-Luxembourg, Brazil, Cameroon, Canada, Chile, China (mainland), Colombia, Costa Rica, Denmark, Dominican Republic, Egypt, El Salvador, Finland, France, Germany, Ghana, Greece, Guatemala, Honduras, Hong Kong, India, Indonesia, Ireland, Israel, Italy, Ivory Coast, Jamaica, Japan, Jordan, Kenya, Malaysia, Mexico, Morocco, Netherlands, New Zealand, Nicaragua, Nigeria, Norway, Pakistan, Panama, Paraguay Philippines, Poland, Portugal, Saudi Arabia, Senegal, Singapore, South African Customs Union (Botswana, Lesotho, Namibia, South Africa, and Swaziland), South Korea, Spain, Sri Lanka, Sweden, Switzerland, Taiwan, Thailand, Trinidad-Tobago, Tunisia, Turkey, United Kingdom, United States, Uruguay, Venezuela, and Zambia.

[16] We assume that empty cells are due to no trade actually having taken place.

[17] The correlation between *MA* and *AA* is high. Classic signs of multicollinearity arose when both *MA* and *AA* variables were included in the same equation. The magnitude, sign, and statistical significance of these variables often changed upon removal of either one of them.

To circumvent such statistical problems, we ran separate equations for (1) trade creation by including MA but not AA and (2) trade diversion by including *AA* but not *MA*.

18 Rejection of the null hypothesis that ñ = 0 confirms the existence of correlation between the output and selection equations.

19 Unfortunately, it was not possible to draw inferences about possible bias associated with missing observations and zero trade in our generalized gravity models. When attempting to apply the Heckman framework to these models, the Hessian became unstable, precluding convergence.

20 According to Rose and van Wincoop and the theoretical underpinnings of the gravity framework identified by Anderson and van Wincoop, the coefficient of a time-invariant coefficient, such as landlockedness, is an estimate of $(\sigma - 1)\ln m$, where $(m - 1)$ is its tariff equivalent and σ is the elasticity of substitution.

21 The percentage change in trade attributable to landlockedness in the benchmark equation is $(e^{\beta 5} - 1) \times 100$.

22 These empirical findings are consistent with results elsewhere. Magee (2008); Eicher and Henn (2009); and Baier and Bergstrand (2007) found that the inclusion of country-pair fixed effects in gravity equations lowered RTA parameter estimates.

23 Neither of these studies addressed the issue of RTA-induced trade contraction.

24 Similarly, agricultural trade creation was also the least for HICs exporting to the set of all importers, rising 40 percent.

25 The term $-\ln(Y_w)$ is common across all countries and is therefore captured through a constant in the regression model. The term $\ln(Y_i) - \ln(P_i)$ is constant across all exporters for a given importer. It is captured by the exporter dummy, (δ_i). The term $\ln(Y_i) - \ln(P_i)$ is constant across all importers for a given exporter. It is captured through the importer dummy, (δ_j).

26 The "trade costs" for exogenous factor m is $p_m = \beta_m / (1-\sigma)$, where is the substitution elasticity.

In: The Influence of Trade Agreements ... ISBN: 978-1-62417-388-2
Editor: Benjamin Stenton

Chapter 3

SELECTED TRADE AGREEMENTS AND IMPLICATIONS FOR U.S. AGRICULTURE*

John Wainio, Mark Gehlhar and John Dyck

ABSTRACT

Since 2001, the United States has concluded negotiations with 13 countries, resulting in 8 trade agreements (TAs). Three additional agreements have been negotiated but not yet ratified by Congress, as of March 2011. Other countries have become increasingly active in negotiating their own trade pacts. This proliferation of TAs between key U.S. trading partners and competitors may have raised concerns among U.S. exporters, whose share in established markets could be eroded by such deals. In this study, ERS examines how recently concluded TAs between ASEAN (Southeast Asia) countries and China and Australia/New Zealand, as well as pending TAs between the United States and Korea, Colombia, and Panama, will likely affect U.S. agricultural trade. Model results suggest that TAs between ASEAN countries and China and ASEAN countries and Australia/ New Zealand would result in moderate losses to U.S. agricultural exports of about $350 million to those countries, but losses would be partially offset by gains in other markets. U.S. agricultural exports to Korea would expand by an estimated $1.9 billion per year if the U.S. TA with Korea were

* This is an edited, reformatted and augmented version of United States Department of Agriculture, Economic Research Service, Economic Research Report 115, dated April 2011.

implemented. The U.S.-Colombia TA would result in an estimated $370 million in additional U.S. exports per year. U.S. exports would realize smaller gains of about $50 million per year under the pact with Panama. Empirical results confirm theoretical findings that trade created under TAs exceeds trade diverted, but that results depend on the specific circumstances of each agreement.

ACKNOWLEDGMENTS

The authors thank Jason Carver, Dylan Daniels, and Olya Lutchyn of USDA's Foreign Agricultural Service; Carol Goodloe of USDA's Office of the Chief Economist; Suchada Langley, Mary Anne Normile, Daniel Pick, and Sally Thompson of USDA's Economic Research Service (ERS); and four anonymous reviewers for their reviews and valuable comments. We also thank John Weber and Cynthia A. Ray of ERS for editorial and design services.

ABBREVIATIONS AND ACRONYMS

AANZFTA	ASEAN-Australia and New Zealand Free Trade Agreement
ASEAN	Association of Southeast Asian Nations
ATPA	Andean Trade Preference Act
BSE	bovine spongiform encephalopathy
CBERA	Caribbean Basin Economic Recovery Act
CDE	constant difference elasticity
CTPA	U.S.-Colombia Trade Promotion Agreement
CRS	constant returns to scale
EFTA	European Free Trade Association
EHP	early harvest program
ERS	Economic Research Service (USDA)
EU	European Union
FTA	free trade agreement
GATT	General Agreement on Tariffs and Trade
GDP	gross domestic product
GSP	Generalized System of Preferences
GTAP	Global Trade Analysis Project
HS	Harmonized System

IDB	WTO integrated database
KORUS	U.S.-Korea Trade Agreement
MERCOSUR	Mercado Común del Sur (Southern Common Market)
MFN	most-favored-nation
NAFTA	North American Free Trade Agreement
NTM	nontariff measure
PTPA	U.S.-Panama Trade Promotion Agreement
SPS	sanitary and phytosanitary
TA	trade agreement
TRQ	tariff-rate quota
USDA	U.S. Department of Agriculture
USITC	U.S. International Trade Commission
USTR	U.S. Trade Representative
WTO	World Trade Organization

SUMMARY

What Is the Issue?

Regional and bilateral free trade agreements (FTAs) have taken on greater significance amidst an evolving international trading environment. Member countries in FTAs agree to eliminate trade barriers on all or most goods and services traded among them. Uncertainties associated with global negotiations under the World Trade Organization (WTO) Doha Development Agenda, along with other factors, have contributed to an upsurge in bilateral and regional trade agreements. In this context, major traders have been pursuing FTAs; the United States has concluded negotiations with 16 countries since 2001, resulting in 8 trade agreements (TAs) with 13 countries. Three additional trade pacts with the Republic of Korea (South Korea, henceforth Korea), Colombia, and Panama have been signed but not yet ratified by the U.S. Congress as of March 2011.

Countries other than the United States are actively negotiating their own trade pacts. Trade agreements between key U.S trading partners and/or competitors may have raised concerns among U.S. exporters, whose ability to maintain share in established markets could be eroded by such agreements, particularly in countries where U.S. competitors have gained preferential access for their products. Korea, Colombia, and the 10 ASEAN (Association of Southeast Asian Nations) countries have been particularly aggressive in negotiating TAs.

In this study, we estimate the possible impacts on U.S. agricultural trade of two recently implemented FTAs in which the United States is not a partner: the FTAs between the ASEAN countries and China and between the ASEAN countries and Australia/New Zealand. We also examine the potential effects on U.S. agricultural exporters of pending bilateral TAs between the United States and Korea, Colombia, and Panama.

What Did the Study Find?

The effect on U.S. agricultural exports resulting from FTAs that exclude the United States depends mainly on the current structure of trade and tariffs in the FTA market and the extent to which tariffs or other barriers are decreased as a result of the FTA. In markets where tariffs levied on U.S. exports will be significantly higher than those levied on FTA members, and where U.S. exporters compete directly with FTA members, the FTA can result in declining U.S. market share. In some cases, however, these losses can be made up by increases in U.S. exports to other markets.

- Model results suggest that U.S. agricultural exports to the ASEAN region would be moderately affected by tariff cuts negotiated under the ASEAN FTAs with China and with Australia/New Zealand. Demand for U.S. exports of bulk commodities, such as wheat, oilseeds, and cotton, would be sustained because these commodities already face low tariffs in the region.
- Although most-favored-nation applied tariffs for ASEAN countries are low in general, pockets of high tariffs remain. Eliminating these could divert ASEAN country trade with non-FTA members toward the FTA partners.
- Overall, U.S. agricultural exports to the ASEAN region are estimated to fall about $350 million per year as a result of the FTAs, equal to about 6 percent of U.S. exports to this region. Much of the decrease would be in processed products, reflecting competition the United States faces from China, Australia, and New Zealand in the ASEAN market. Some U.S. exports may be diverted to other markets, offsetting some of the decrease in trade with ASEAN countries. As a

result, global U.S. agricultural exports are estimated to decline by only 0.1 percent, or about $173 million per year.

Pending bilateral TAs between the United States and Korea, Colombia, and Panama have potential mutual benefits.

- U.S. agriculture will benefit from pending TAs between the United States and Korea, Colombia, and Panama, largely because U.S. exports to these markets currently face significantly higher tariffs than exports from these countries face in the U.S. market.
- Of the three pending U.S. TAs, the U.S.-Korea Trade Agreement (KORUS) would offer the largest gains for U.S. agriculture. Total U.S. agricultural export gains in the Korean market are estimated at over $1.9 billion annually, an increase of about 40 percent. The U.S.-Colombia Trade Promotion Agreement (CTPA) is estimated to generate an increase of 44 percent in U.S. exports, or an additional $370 million per year. Though Panama represents a relatively small market, the U.S.- Panama Trade Promotion Agreement (PTPA) is expected to provide U.S. exporters with opportunities for an additional $46 million in annual sales of rice, corn, meats, dairy, and processed foods.
- Each pending U.S. TA partner would have additional access to the U.S. market for those agricultural commodities that now face U.S. tariff-rate quotas. The U.S. sugar sector would face competition from increased imports of sugar from Colombia and Panama. Ethnic foods, such as biscuits, savory snack foods, ramen noodles, and seaweed products, would account for the bulk of the small increase in additional imports from Korea as a result of KORUS. Other imports from the three countries could be accommodated by the large U.S. market with little effect on domestic prices or production.

How Was the Study Conducted?

The analysis of FTAs in this report uses the most current and comprehensive WTO tariff submissions. Applied tariffs were matched to trade flow values from official country customs data to provide a preliminary assessment of the extent to which the United States would face greater competition from competing exporters in selected markets. Measures of tariff protection estimated for both the United States and its trading partners and for the ASEAN countries and their new FTA partners were based on the actual negotiated reductions in tariffs for each FTA and used to quantify the impacts of each free trade agreement. The study employed a well-known global modeling framework (Global Trade Analysis Project) to assess the impacts on agricultural trade.

INTRODUCTION

In March 2001, Robert Zoellick, then U.S. Trade Representative, unveiled the Bush administration's trade strategy of negotiating multilateral, regional, and bilateral trade agreements, placing the United States at the heart of a network of initiatives to open markets (Blustein, 2009).[1] The strategy was grounded in two fundamental ideas: (1) trade liberalization is beneficial to the U.S. economy, and (2) each venue for trade liberalization offers unique opportunities (Burfisher and Zahniser, 2003). The U.S. strategy resulted in the initiation of bilateral and regional trade negotiations with over 40 countries, resulting in 8 trade agreements (TAs) with 13 countries.[2] Three additional trade agreements with the Republic of Korea (South Korea, henceforth Korea), Colombia, and Panama were signed by each country but not yet ratified by the U.S. Congress as of March 2011.[3] For many reasons, the World Trade Organization (WTO) Doha round of multilateral trade negotiations has not yielded timely results. Instead, the uncertainties associated with these talks, and other factors, have motivated countries to negotiate their own bilateral and regional pacts. The lack of progress by the WTO and the rush to sign free trade agreements (FTAs) may actually have become mutually supporting, with one feeding off the other. Certainly, FTAs are now the most prominent and rapidly expanding feature of the multilateral trading system. The number of FTAs, as well as the share of world trade that takes place among FTA partners, has steadily increased—from fewer than 25 FTAs in 1990 to 290 in 2010—a trend likely to be strengthened by the many FTAs currently under negotiation. In 2009, trade between FTA partners accounted for an estimated 45 percent of global nonagricultural trade and 54 percent of global agricultural trade. For the United States, these proportions were 33 percent and 41 percent, respectively, which demonstrates that, despite early U.S. efforts to negotiate TAs with trading partners, these agreements still account for a smaller portion of U.S. trade than for world trade as a whole.[4] The popularity of FTAs is largely tied to their potential for expanding trade between members as consumers respond to the availability of lower priced imports. At the same time, these agreements are by definition discriminatory, which can lead to trade being diverted from nonmembers to members. U.S. agricultural exporters' ability to maintain market share in numerous countries that have recently signed FTAs with U.S. competitors is in question. Given the significance of overseas markets to U.S. agriculture, coupled with the rapid expansion of "third-country" FTAs, it is important that U.S. exporters understand how these agreements may affect their ability to compete in the future. At the center of the debate surrounding third-country FTAs is the potential for trade diversion. Trade diversion refers to the diversion of trade from relatively efficient nonmembers to relatively inefficient members. In contrast, trade creation is the result of factors such as lower consumer prices and greater choices and can involve a shift of production from inefficient domestic providers to more efficient FTA partners. The broad picture that emerges in both the theoretical and empirical literature on FTAs is that trade creation tends to be the rule, trade diversion the exception (Freund and Ornelas, 2010). This may be related to the fact that most countries tend to form their first FTAs with "natural trading partners,"—neighboring countries or countries in their region—with which they already have an established trading relationship.[5] Krugman (1991) demonstrated that where FTAs are formed by natural partners with low trade costs, the gains from freeing intraregional trade are large and trade creation dominates over trade diversion. Trade agreements exhibiting these characteristics include the EU, NAFTA, MERCOSUR, ASEAN, and EFTA (see abbreviations and acronyms, p. iii). These regional pacts have also been among the most studied FTAs, and although the results from these studies are not necessarily applicable to all FTAs, the trade creation and trade diversion outcomes from these large agreements dominate the results from studies that measure trade effects across all FTAs. The salient point is that, while overall trade diversion does not appear to be a major concern in the economic literature, in some agreements and sectors it can be significant. In recent years, countries that have exhausted regional prospects have begun looking further afield for preferential partners. It is entirely plausible that these FTAs will result in a higher level of trade diversion. In this study, we use a global trade model to estimate the possible effects of two recently implemented third-country FTAs on U.S. agricultural trade:

- The FTA between ASEAN countries and China
- The FTA between ASEAN countries and Australia/New Zealand[6]

The ASEAN countries have been a growing market for U.S. agricultural exports; hence, there is strong interest in determining how these two FTAs might affect the United States. To shed light on which individual U.S. products might be vulnerable to trade diversion, we also take a more detailed look at trade flows and the margins of preference between the United States and FTA members, measured as the difference between the tariff that U.S. exports will face after the FTAs have been fully implemented and the tariff the FTA members receive within the FTAs.

Despite pressure to protect the interests of U.S. producers of import-sensitive commodities (see box, "Key Agricultural Issues in FTAs"), U.S. agricultural organizations and food industry associations tend to view FTAs as a way to create opportunities to increase agricultural exports by lowering and possibly eliminating tariffs. Increasing exports is viewed as vital to improving farm income and business profitability.

As mentioned, the United States negotiated three TAs that have yet to be implemented as of March 2011. The United States and Colombia formally signed the Colombia Trade Promotion Agreement (CTPA) on November 22, 2006.

A month later, on December 19, 2006, U.S. and Panamanian negotiators reached agreement on a comprehensive trade agreement, the Panama Trade Promotion Agreement (PTPA). The following year, on June 30, 2007, the United States and Korea signed the U.S.-Korea TA (commonly referred to as KORUS). Before each of these TAs can take effect, Congress must approve the implementing legislation submitted by the President.

Key Agricultural Issues in FTAs

The coverage of agriculture in free trade agreements (FTAs) often reflects the situation prevailing at the multilateral level, with the same products resistant to liberalization at the multilateral level also excluded from liberalization within FTAs. The coverage of nonagricultural products in FTAs, when measured as a share of tariff lines, is substantially higher for most agreements than coverage of agricultural products, confirming that liberalizing agricultural trade is no easier for countries at the regional level than it is at the multilateral level (WTO, 2009).

Most countries, including the United States, have some agricultural products that benefit from high levels of border protection. In many cases, it has proved difficult for partner countries to reduce barriers for these import-sensitive products within an FTA.

Trade agreements (TAs) negotiated by the United States have generally been comprehensive in scope, sometimes to the point of including unfettered market access for sensitive agricultural products. The sections dealing with the agricultural provisions in pending U.S. TAs with Korea, Colombia, and Panama provide details on treatment of sensitive products under each agreement.

As they are included within legally binding agreements, FTA tariff commitments not only provide for the reduction and elimination of tariffs but also provide assurance that these tariffs will not be subsequently increased. These FTA bindings are particularly valuable in agriculture, where World Trade Organization (WTO) bound tariffs can be extremely high on some products, even though the most-favored-nation (MFN) applied tariffs are much lower.[1] Because multilateral tariff negotiations are done on the basis of a country's bound, or maximum allowable, tariffs, increases in market access as a result of negotiated tariff reductions only occur when the new bound tariff drops below the applied tariff. In the case of tariff cuts negotiated under FTAs, however, the first tariff cut is often made off a recent applied rate rather than the bound one. As a result, FTAs can have very immediate trade impacts.

In addition to addressing agricultural tariffs, countries often seek to address nontariff barriers in FTAs, particularly sanitary and phytosanitary (SPS) measures applied in the food safety and animal/ plant health areas. Although the United States has not normally used TAs as a mechanism to address the substance of SPS issues in the past, sanitary issues related to U.S. beef exports were particularly important in the negotiation of the Korea, Colombia, and Panama TAs (Jurenas, 2009).

The Colombia TA contains an SPS side letter addressing the terms of access under which U.S. beef and beef products would be allowed to enter Colombia. In the case of the Panama TA, both governments have signed an agreement detailing how SPS measures and technical standards will be applied to bilateral agricultural trade. Panama agreed to accept the U.S. meat and poultry inspection system "as equivalent to its own" and provide access for all U.S. beef and poultry on the basis of accepted international standards.

In the Korea TA, the terms of access for U.S. beef were particularly contentious. At the time the negotiations were concluded, all differences had not been resolved both to increase market access for U.S. beef and to address Korea's human health concerns.

Subsequent negotiations led to the announcement of a "voluntary private sector arrangement" on June 21, 2008, that limits sales to U.S. beef only from cattle less than 30 months old. While both countries are said to view this as a transitional step intended to improve Korean consumer confidence in U.S. beef, the issue remains politically sensitive in both countries. U.S. efforts to persuade Korea to accept U.S. beef from cattle of all ages remain unresolved as of this report's release.

[1] WTO bound tariffs are ceiling commitments made by members to hold duties beneath an agreed level. Once a tariff is bound under the WTO, it may not be raised above the bound level without compensating the affected parties. In practice, the actual tariff a country applies on imports may be at or below the bound rate. These are called most-favored-nation (MFN) applied rates. Each WTO member must grant this rate to all other WTO members under the GATT's (General Agreement on Tariffs and Trade) MFN rule. MFN treatment is aimed at preventing WTO members from discriminating between trading partners. In some cases, however, the WTO allows a country to charge some of its trading partners a rate below the MFN applied tariff. These rates, called preferential tariffs, include the tariffs negotiated under FTAs.

Shortly after each TA was negotiated, the U.S. International Trade Commission (USITC) published assessments of the likely effect of each agreement on the U.S. economy as a whole and on specific industry sectors, including agriculture. Since these reports were released, there have been significant changes in the global economy and in international relations. Colombia, in particular, has been active in negotiating additional FTAs with some key U.S. competitors. One of these FTAs—with the four members of MERCOSUR (Argentina, Brazil, Paraguay, and Uruguay)—has already had visible effects on U.S. agricultural exports and market shares in the Colombian market. The U.S. market position in the Colombian market may soon be further eroded if the Canada-Colombia FTA and the EU-Colombia FTA enter into force and competing exports from these countries receive duty-free treatment. Likewise, Korea is negotiating FTAs with the EU, MERCOSUR, and Australia. All of these countries are major competitors with the United States in the Korean market. To maintain and improve their competitive position relative to that of third countries, U.S. producers will also need duty-free access to these markets. We use the GTAP global trade model to explore the significance to U.S. agricultural exporters of implementing the pending U.S. TAs with Korea and Colombia. Differences between ERS GTAP model results and those of the USITC reflect the use of different model assumptions and base years. We also analyze U.S-Panama trade flows and tariff commitments under the pending U.S. TA with Panama to identify agricultural products that may benefit from duty-free treatment and report the gains from implementing the TA calculated by the USITC.

MODEL, DATA, AND ASSUMPTIONS

In this study, we employ a multiregion computable general equilibrium model known as GTAP (Global Trade Analysis Project). The primary advantage of GTAP is that it incorporates explicit bilateral trade flows, which allows for the analysis of free trade agreements (see box, "The GTAP Framework"). Each TA, except the U.S.-Panama TA, was analyzed separately to measure the long-term effects of a one-time, full implementation of individual agreements.

The FTA final tariffs and tariff-rate quotas (TRQ) used in the GTAP model were obtained from the final texts of each of the FTAs. The applied MFN tariffs were obtained from the WTO's Integrated Database (IDB). The margins of preference were calculated as the difference between the applied MFN tariffs on U.S. exports and the tariffs to be levied on the exports of FTA partners after the FTAs are fully implemented. The U.S. export and import data were obtained from USITC's Dataweb. Trade data for other countries were obtained through the Global Trade Information Service's World Trade Atlas database.

The GTAP simulations were implemented by applying the reductions or eliminations of the import tariff rates that were agreed upon in each FTA. A few assumptions deserve note. The GTAP database reflects the applied tariff rates in 2004, including applied tariffs on trade between ASEAN members. It was assumed that ASEAN members would attain duty-free access to each other's markets by 2009, with the exception of trade in rice. To update tariffs, it was necessary to eliminate those tariffs on trade between ASEAN members prior to extending the FTA with nonmembers of ASEAN. In the case of pending TAs, it is uncertain as to when these agreements would be implemented. It was assumed that implementation of the agreements would begin by 2014.

FTAs often allow for long implementation periods in the reduction of tariff rates, in some cases as long as 20 years. In this study, the transition periods are ignored, and the reductions in protection simply assume the full change in tariffs after the transition period. While this will yield effects that reflect fully implemented tariff cuts, this approach does not provide a time path of the effects of these FTAs into the future. Rather, the results were obtained using a comparative static framework and are an attempt to simulate trade flows in the base period under a new set of tariffs. We know, however, that economic growth could arise from trade liberalization over time. The static nature of the model we used does not generate results that reflect the dynamic gains of trade liberalization. These are effects that could accrue through increased savings and investment, increasing returns to scale, or improvements in factor productivity through technological spillovers or through freeing up the importation of intermediate and capital goods. All of these additional channels of economic growth can magnify the static effects of trade liberalization.

The GTAP Framework

The Global Trade Analysis Project (GTAP) framework consists of a publically documented model and global database (Hertel and Tsigas, 1997; Narayanan and Walmsley, 2008). The model links national income accounts of all countries through trade and investment flows. The framework provides comprehensive coverage of production, consumption, and trade of all goods and services. Aspects of the model include a global banking sector, which intermediates between global savings and consumption. Domestic products and imports are consumed by firms, governments, and households. The model imposes both theoretical and basic accounting consistency conditions at the national and global level. For example, income by households is derived from returns to factors and is used for either consumption or savings. In this study, we adopt standard assumptions for the model. The model uses a constant difference elasticity (CDE) demand system for representing private household preferences. The model assumes that consumers maximize utility subject to a budget constraint and that producers maximize profits by combining intermediate inputs and primary factors at least possible cost. Within each region, firms produce output by employing labor and capital and intermediate inputs. Land, however, is employed only in agricultural sectors. Constant returns to scale (CRS) is assumed for all production sectors. Firm output is purchased by consumers, governments, other firms, and by other countries as exports. It is assumed that capital and labor are fully mobile within regions.

Product markets are assumed to be perfectly competitive, implying zero economic profit for the firm. Imports are assumed as imperfect substitutes for domestic products and differentiated by origin using an Armington-type specification. The standard model is used to perform comparative static analysis where it is assumed that sufficient time is allowed for all markets to adjust to a new equilibrium. Capital accumulation is allowed based upon a Baldwin-type specification as described by Francois et al. (1996). The model is solved as a system of equations using the GEMPACK software (Harrison and Pearson, 1996). The most recent publically available release of the GTAP data (Version 7) is benchmarked to the year 2004. Ideally, the benchmark year should coincide with the period in which implementation takes place. In this study, the GTAP benchmark year for pending free trade agreements (TAs) was updated to 2014 (see app. 1).

As with all models, the GTAP framework has some limitations. Being a comparative static model, it does not capture many of the dynamic effects from increased trade or increased foreign investment. In addition, it provides no explicit time dimension for estimating when effects from an FTA may arise. The impacts reflect what the model's base year might have looked like under a different set of policies. We know, however, that the effects of trade liberalization take time to unfold. Dynamic models capture these longterm gains of trade liberalization by accounting for increased savings and investment and improvements in factor productivity from better resource allocation, deepening specialization, and technology spillovers. All of these additional channels of economic growth can magnify the static gains of trade liberalization.

The model structure also does not allow for potentially new trade flows, or extensive margin trade, where trade in the base year is zero. Nor does it account for nontariff measures (NTMs), such as sanitary and phytosanitary measures or technical barriers to trade. In some cases, zero trade in the base year is a function of NTMs, so cutting tariffs would not necessarily result in new trade flows. Some of these FTAs address some of these measures through the creation of a Standing Committee on Sanitary and Phytosanitary Matters in an effort to avoid or resolve trade problems generated by these measures. To the extent that an FTA results in reducing NTMs through the harmonization of technical barriers such as labeling, recognizing equivalence in each other's food safety regimes, or mutually agreeing to suspend antidumping laws, these reductions would not be captured in our analysis.

Finally, the model data are historical, which can misrepresent current trade patterns. In the analysis of the pending U.S. TAs with Korea and Colombia, the model values were projected to 2014, when the TAs are assumed to have taken effect, based on current economic trends as described in appendix 1.

THE ASEAN FTAS WITH CHINA AND AUSTRALIA/ NEW ZEALAND

The FTAs implemented in recent years between ASEAN and China and ASEAN and Australia and New Zealand (henceforth, Oceania) reduce trade barriers among major agricultural trading nations that have strong agricultural trade ties to the United States. The trade profiles of the three entities (ASEAN, China, Oceania) have some overlaps but also strong differences; the three regions specialize in different kinds of agricultural trade. Summaries of the entities follow.

- *ASEAN* is a net exporting region for agricultural trade, but its agricultural imports are large and growing. ASEAN is also a net agricultural exporter to the United States, with U.S. imports from ASEAN exceeding exports by over $1 billion in each year during 2005-08. ASEAN exports to the world (and to the United States) span a wide range of products, including rubber, palm and coconut oil, rice, cocoa, pineapples, bananas, coffee, cashews, and spices. In most cases, these products do not compete with U.S. agricultural products; rice and vegetable oils are the chief exceptions. ASEAN imports wheat, corn, soybeans, soymeal, distillers' dried grains, dairy products, fruits, and processed agricultural products in large quantities.
- *China* is a net agricultural importing country. In 2009, it had agricultural imports of about $45 billion and agricultural exports of about $25 billion. Vegetables and fruits (often processed) and other processed food products dominate China's exports, which are often relatively labor-intensive products. Exports to the United States include processed vegetables (such as mushrooms, water chestnuts, garlic, and soy products); processed fruits (led by tangerines); apple juice; pet food; and sausage casings. U.S. exports to China are

considerably larger than U.S. imports from China: $13 billion versus $3 billion in 2009. At a value of over $9 billion per year, U.S. soybean exports dominate agricultural trade between the two countries. Cotton, poultry products, and distillers' dried grains are among the other large U.S. exports to China.

- *Australia and New Zealand (Oceania)* are large net exporters, together exporting $33 billion in agricultural products and importing $9 billion in 2009. Australia exports wheat, barley, cotton, and other crops. Both countries export large amounts of pasture-based animal products: beef, lamb, and mutton; dairy products; and wool. Wine exports are also important. U.S. imports from Oceania (beef, lamb, dairy products, and wine), at $2.5 billion, are considerably larger than U.S. exports to the region ($1.1 billion in 2009), which are led by pork, pet food, and grapes.

As an agricultural exporter, the United States competes in all three markets (ASEAN, China, Oceania). When U.S competitors in these markets receive lower tariffs on their exports, U.S. exports will be affected to some extent. For example, under an initial agreement between ASEAN and China that was signed in 2002 and took effect on January 1, 2004, ASEAN tariffs declined on apples from China. U.S. apple exports to ASEAN have since decreased whereas China's apple exports have increased (see box, "The Early Harvest Between ASEAN and China").

The Early Harvest between ASEAN and China

China and the ASEAN (Association of Southeast Nations) countries agreed in Brunei in 2001 to establish a free trade area within 10 years. In a subsequent meeting in Phnom Penh, Cambodia, in 2002, the parties set up an Early Harvest program that would eliminate tariffs on goods in the first eight chapters of the Harmonized System by 2010 among members of the new FTA. These chapters cover live animals, meat and edible meat offal, fish, dairy products and eggs, other animal products, live plants, vegetables, and fruits.

Tariffs on products within these chapters were to be reduced or brought to zero for trade between China and a wealthier group within ASEAN, comprising Singapore, Brunei, Indonesia, Thailand, the Philippines, and Malaysia (ASEAN 6).

Countries could choose to exclude a limited number of specific commodities from the Early Harvest and could substantially reduce tariffs, rather than completely eliminate them. The other ASEAN countries agreed to more limited trade liberalization. Most of the tariff reductions appear to have been carried out.

U.S. fruit exports may have been seriously affected by the tariff reductions granted to China's fruit exports in the Early Harvest. In 1997, U.S. apple exports to Southeast Asia peaked at 150,000 tons, just as the Asian financial crisis struck. The crisis led to sharp devaluations of Southeast Asian currencies that raised the prices of imported apples and income losses that further discouraged apple buying, triggering a dramatic decrease in U.S. apple exports to the region. However, when incomes rebounded in the mid-2000s and Southeast Asian currencies were stronger, U.S. exports failed to increase. Increased apple imports by the region were largely captured by exports from China (see figure). Tariff reductions granted on imports of Chinese apples under the Early Harvest likely contributed to the shift to exports from China. Tariffs levied on imports of U.S. apples are now higher than those on Chinese apples everywhere in the region, except in Singapore and Brunei. In the most important markets, the difference in tariffs is 5-10 percent. Thai imports of apples from China doubled in the first year (2003) in which 10-percent tariffs previously facing China were removed. Grapes, another leading U.S. export to the region, have also lost market share. Tariffs on grape imports from the United States are as high as 30 percent, while tariffs on imports from China are now zero in all the ASEAN countries.

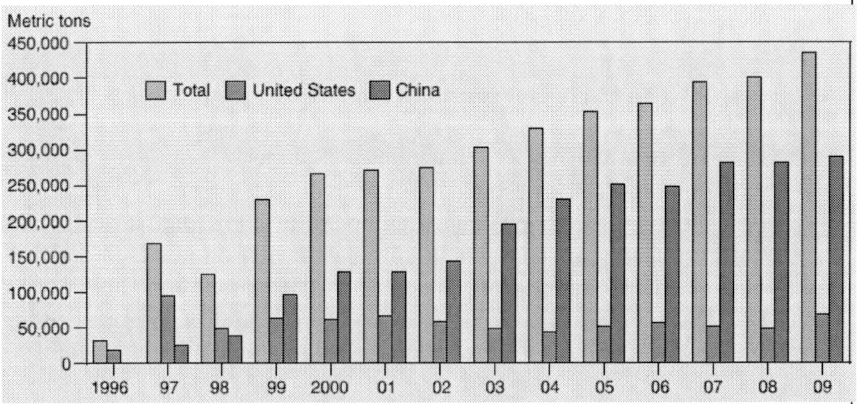

Note: Southeast Asia data are for Indonesia, Malaysia, Philippines, Singapore, and Thailand.

Source: USDA, Economic Research Service using official import data in the Global Trade Atlas.

Apple imports by Southeast Asia.

The ASEAN-China free trade area took full effect on January 1, 2010. The final agreement removes tariffs on about 90 percent of goods traded between China and the six founding members of ASEAN (Brunei, Indonesia, Malaysia, the Philippines, Singapore, and Thailand). The agreement with China is scheduled to extend to the other four ASEAN nations—Cambodia, Laos, Burma (Myanmar), and Vietnam—by 2015 (see app. 2, table 1 for information on the agricultural tariff commitments in each agreement). Tariffs for products designated as "sensitive" are to be phased out over a longer term through 2018, while tariffs on "highly sensitive" products will be reduced but not phased out (app. 2, table 2). Under the terms of the FTA, highly sensitive products cannot make up more than 40 percent of the sensitive lines or 100 items at the Harmonized System (HS) six-digit level, whichever is lower.[7] Vietnam and Cambodia were given special extended tariff phase-out provisions for a select group of products.

Australia and New Zealand began jointly negotiating a free trade agreement (AANZFTA) with the ASEAN countries in 2004; the agreement was signed in 2009 and entered into force in April 2010. Australia and New Zealand will benefit from the eventual elimination of tariffs on 99 percent of their exports to the ASEAN countries. Some tariffs were eliminated immediately, with the majority of the remaining tariffs reaching zero at various stages between 2011 and 2020 (app. 2, table 2). A few tariffs will not reach zero until 2025. About 5 percent of the ASEAN countries' tariffs will not be cut to zero. The ASEAN countries, on the other hand, will be granted duty-free access in Australia and New Zealand for all agricultural goods by 2020.

ASEAN's regional free trade agreements are complex:

- The FTAs with China and Oceania do not provide uniform treatment across all ASEAN members. Each ASEAN country has its own schedule of reductions on import barriers.
- The FTAs also vary widely across the commodity spectrum. Some products, such as rice, receive no bilateral tariff reduction in some or all of the national-level schedules of reduction. The "level of ambition" of the agreements is not aimed at wholly free bilateral trade in either of these agreements.
- The FTAs are implemented on different schedules for each country, and the phase-in also differs by commodity within each country. Some commodity tariffs go to zero in the first year of implementation, while others are reduced to zero only after more than 20 years.

Products with no close domestic substitute tend to see faster reductions.

- Some countries retain TRQs even with the new FTA partners. The concession under the FTA is often to reduce the in-quota tariff over a period of time for the new partner.

Potential Impact on U.S. Agricultural Exports

U.S. agricultural exports to the partners in the new ASEAN-related FTAs were about $20 billion in 2009 (table 1). Of this amount, almost half were soybean exports, of which China alone accounted for $9 billion. Cotton and oilseed products represented another 12 percent of the total. Altogether, oilseeds and oilseed products and cotton constituted over 60 percent of total U.S. agricultural exports to the three regions. Import barriers to oilseeds and cotton are low worldwide because these commodities are used as inputs by industries that governments are trying to promote (i.e., meat and textiles). ASEAN, China, and Oceania are no exception; tariffs on oilseeds, oilseed products, and cotton are generally low, and often zero. Hence, much of U.S. agricultural trade going across the Pacific faced low tariffs before the ASEAN FTAs were implemented and, thus, would not be significantly affected by the agreements. Furthermore, U.S. exports of some major commodities, such as soybeans and distillers' dried grains, would face little competition with exports from China (the world's largest importer), ASEAN (major importers), or Oceania (net importers).

This analysis focuses on Indonesia, Thailand, the Philippines, Malaysia, and Vietnam. The rest of ASEAN's members are excluded from much of the analysis because of their small size or lack of data. Singapore has free trade for virtually all its imports. Brunei has a small economy and very small agricultural trade. Multilateral trade data are difficult to obtain for Burma, Cambodia, and Laos.

As shown in figure 1, the amount of trade that might be vulnerable to heightened competition as a result of these FTAs would appear to be substantially less than the total. The bar on the bottom of each figure displays the 5-year average value of agricultural goods imported from the United States between 2005 and 2009.[8] The bar above it displays the portion of imports from the United States that competed with exports from at least one of the FTA partners in at least 1 of the 5 years.[9] In the case of the four ASEAN countries depicted, this is the portion of U.S. trade that competed directly with trade from China and Oceania; in the case of China, Australia, and New Zealand, it represents the portion of U.S. trade that competed with ASEAN exports to these countries. The top three bars in the figures apportion the competing exports by the amount that faced zero tariffs, tariffs of 5 percent or less, and tariffs greater than 5 percent. We used 2006 MFN applied rates for each country except Australia as a proxy for tariffs faced by the United States during the entire period. For Australia, we used the tariffs faced by the United States under the U.S.-Australia FTA.

Table 1. U.S. agricultural exports to ASEAN FTA partners, 2009

	ASEAN	China	Australia-New Zealand	Total
			$ millions	
Wheat	693	87	0	779
Rice	11	1	38	49
Other grains	42	48	0	90
Oilseeds	1,134	9,214	32	10,380
Cotton	619	862	1	1,481
Fruits and vegetables	387	178	211	777
Oilseed products	824	92	97	1,013
Poultry, pork, and offal	238	446	124	808
Beef and offal	201	1	3	205
Dairy products	291	137	27	455
Processed foods	633	267	260	1,160
Other agriculture	1,137	1,779	279	3,196
Total agriculture	6,209	13,112	1,073	20,394

ASEAN = Association of Southeast Asian Nations. FTA = free trade agreement.
Source: USDA, Economic Research Service using USDA's Foreign Agricultural Trade of the United States database.

In the case of the four ASEAN countries, almost all U.S. trade faced some competition from at least one of the countries' new FTA partners (China, Australia, or New Zealand). In the case of Indonesia and Malaysia, however, a large portion of this trade was imported at MFN applied rates that were set at zero. An estimated 77 percent of Indonesia's agricultural imports from the United States and 69 percent of Malaysia's imports from the United States entered duty free. In the case of Thailand, 37 percent of U.S. exports entered duty free; in the Philippines, all U.S. imports were assessed a duty.

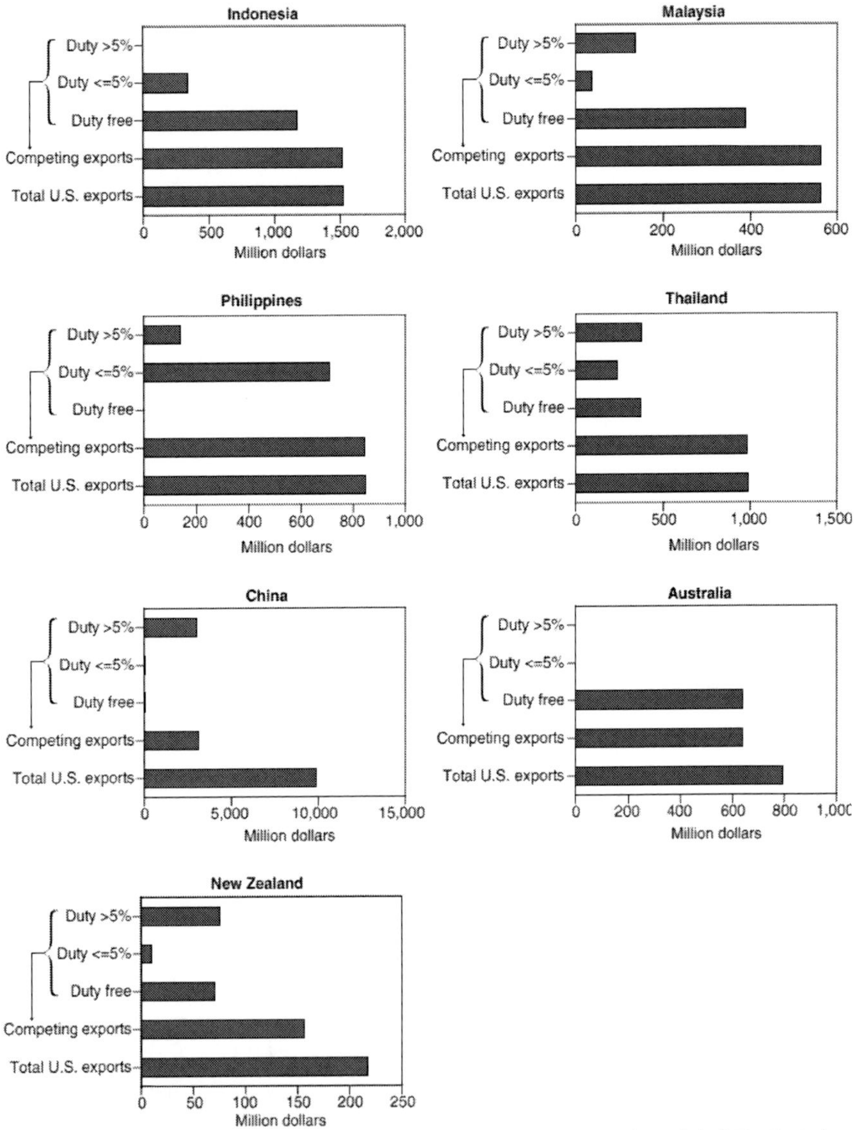

Source: USDA, Economic Research Service using trade data in the Global Trade Atlas and tariff data in ERS databases.

Figure 1. U.S. agricultural exports by size of tariff faced, 2005-09 average.

The annual average level of dutiable U.S. exports to these countries was \$350 million in Indonesia, \$175 million in Malaysia, \$845 million in the

Philippines, and $620 million in Thailand. Focusing only on the portion of U.S. exports subject to duty, we observe that most U.S. exports to Indonesia entered at rates under 5 percent—only 3 percent of dutiable exports from the United States to Indonesia were assessed a tariff of over 5 percent. Although all U.S. agricultural exports to the Philippines were dutiable, only 16 percent were levied a duty above 5 percent. In Malaysia and Thailand, by contrast, the shares were 79 and 61 percent, respectively.

In the case of China, only about a third of U.S. exports faced competition from ASEAN countries, compared with 81 percent in Australia and 72 percent in New Zealand.[10] The majority of U.S. exports to China that competed with exports of ASEAN countries faced tariffs in excess of 5 percent, while U.S. exports to Australia enter duty free under the U.S.- Australia FTA. About 88 percent of the $85 million of dutiable U.S. exports to New Zealand that competed with ASEAN country exports faced tariffs above 5 percent.

Across the seven countries represented in figure 1, U.S. exports averaged $15 billion per year during 2005-09. Of this amount, $7 billion did not compete with exports from the new FTA partners and another $2.66 billion entered duty free, leaving just over $5 billion of dutiable competing exports.

Changes in U.S. Agricultural Exports to the FTA Members

With 2009 trade values as a benchmark, GTAP model results suggest that overall U.S. agricultural exports to the ASEAN region would be mildly affected from implementing these tariff cuts, falling by about 6 percent in total, or just under $350 million per year (table 2). However, effects would vary significantly across ASEAN countries and commodities (table 3). These differences largely reflect the level of direct competition the United States would face from China, Australia, and New Zealand as a result of the improved market access for these countries in the ASEAN region. The breakout for the large ASEAN countries indicates that Thailand would account for over 40 percent of the U.S. export loss. Thai tariffs tend to be the highest among ASEAN's large countries. Indonesia, with generally low tariffs, would see a much smaller per year drop ($21 million) in U.S. exports.

Table 2. Impact on total U.S. agricultural exports from ASEAN FTAs with China, Australia, and New Zealand[1]

	ASEAN	China	Rest of world	Total
		Percent change		
Wheat	-5.9	1.9	0.2	-0.6
Oilseeds	-1.0	0.5	0.2	0.3
Cotton	-0.4	2.3	-0.5	0.2
Fruits and vegetables	-17.4	-13.8	0.1	-0.6
Oilseed products	1.2	-1.5	0.6	0.6
Poultry, pork, and offal	-22.1	-0.0	0.3	-0.4
Beef and offal	-13.9	1.2	0.4	0.3
Dairy	-16.9	2.1	0.5	-1.9
Processed foods	-11.8	-2.6	0.1	-0.6
Other agriculture	-4.5	0.3	0.1	0.0
Total agriculture	-6.2	0.5	0.2	-0.1
	ASEAN	China	Rest of world	Total
		$ millions		
Wheat	-39.8	1.6	7.5	-30.7
Oilseeds	-10.8	47.5	15.5	52.2
Cotton	-2.8	18.8	-9.3	6.8
Fruits and vegetables	-51.7	-29.9	12.1	-69.5
Oilseed products	9.5	-1.7	32.8	40.6
Poultry, pork, and offal	-54.8	-0.3	20.1	-35.0
Beef and offal	-6.3	0.4	15.9	10.0
Dairy	-43.2	2.5	6.6	-34.1
Processed foods	-123.6	-26.1	26.7	-123.0
Other agriculture	-24.2	3.6	30.4	9.8
Total agriculture	-347.7	16.5	158.2	-173.0

ASEAN = Association of Southeast Asian Nations. FTA = free trade agreement.

[1] Model base year is 2004; dollar amounts are from applying model's percent change to 2009 trade.

Source: USDA, Economic Research Service results of Global Trade Analysis Project modeling exercise for this study.

As a result of tariff cuts, total agricultural exports to ASEAN by Australia and New Zealand would increase by about 27 percent, or nearly $1.2 billion per year. However, their agricultural exports to the rest of the world would fall about 1.6 percent, or $490 billion per year. As products from Australia and New Zealand rise in price, they become less competitive in the rest of the world. Overall agricultural exports from Australia and New Zealand to the world would increase by just 2 percent. U.S. agricultural exports to Oceania would be virtually unchanged, but U.S. agricultural imports from the region would fall by about $50 million per year, mainly due to diversion of beef and dairy products to ASEAN markets.

Table 3. Projected impact on U.S. exports to selected ASEAN countries from FTAs with China, Australia, and New Zealand

	Indonesia	Malaysia	Philippines	Thailand	Vietnam	ASEAN
			Percent change			
Wheat	-7.9	3.2	-6.4	-4.3	-17.7	-5.9
Oilseeds	0.7	-1.0	-4.7	-2.2	-12.3	-1.0
Cotton	1.6	1.1	4.3	-8.6	3.8	-0.4
Fruits and vegetables	-4.9	-3.2	-24.0	-32.8	-35.2	-17.4
Oilseed products	1.8	1.4	0.3	-0.6	3.3	1.2
Poultry, pork, and offal	0.5	-0.1	-36.8	-33.9	-17.7	-22.1
Beef and offal	-13.9	1.2	-6.9	-91.4	-52.2	-13.9
Dairy	-10.3	-0.1	-12.0	-23.7	-41.4	-16.9
Processed foods	-2.5	-4.1	-3.5	-35.6	-14.8	-11.8
Other agriculture	-1.1	-8.9	0.5	-7.7	-5.8	-4.5
Total agriculture	-1.2	-2.3	-7.0	-13.9	-9.6	-6.2
	Indonesia	Malaysia	Philippines	Thailand	Vietnam	ASEAN
			$ millions			
Wheat	-12.0	1.2	-20.5	-6.6	-1.9	-39.8
Oilseeds	4.1	-1.6	-1.2	-4.6	-7.5	-10.8
Cotton	3.7	0.4	0.8	-14.3	6.6	-2.8
Fruits and vegetables	-3.8	-2.2	-11.5	-15.4	-18.8	-51.7
Oilseed products	3.2	1.1	1.1	-0.4	4.6	9.5
Poultry, pork, and offal	0.3	-0.0	-39.3	-1.4	-14.4	-54.8
Beef and offal	-0.8	0.0	-2.3	-0.5	-2.7	-6.3
Dairy	-6.8	-0.1	-9.3	-5.6	-21.4	-43.2
Processed foods	-7.2	-8.3	-8.0	-87.6	-12.5	-123.6
Other agriculture	-1.3	-6.2	0.5	-9.9	-7.4	-24.2
Total agriculture	-20.6	-15.7	-89.6	-146.3	-75.5	-347.7

ASEAN = Association of Southeast Asian Nations. FTA = free trade agreement.

[1] Model base year is 2004; dollar amounts are from applying model's percent change to 2009 trade.

Source: USDA, Economic Research Service results of Global Trade Analysis Project modeling exercise for this study.

U.S. agricultural exports to China are expected to increase marginally, by $16.5 million per year. New tariff preferences for ASEAN are likely to reduce U.S. competitiveness and trade in fruits and vegetables and in processed foods.

However, China's demand for oilseeds and cotton is expected to increase because of growth in its livestock and textile sectors as a result of the ASEAN FTA, raising demand for more imported inputs.

Under this scenario, U.S. exports to the rest of the world would likely increase; as trade intensifies among the three FTA regions, existing exports to nonparticipating parts of the world by these countries would be in shorter supply and more expensive. U.S. agriculture would gain, marginally, in other markets. With a gain of over $150 million in new trade to balance against the loss in trade to ASEAN, U.S. agricultural exports to the world would drop approximately $173 million after implementation of the FTAs.

Identifying U.S. Exports Most Vulnerable to Increased Competition

This section takes a more disaggregated look at those U.S. products most vulnerable to increased competition in China, Australia, New Zealand, and ASEAN. We concentrate only on those U.S. products in each country that competed with products from at least one country that was a new FTA partner and that were charged a duty (the trade represented in the top two bars in figure 1). To simplify the analysis, we focus only on tariff lines where U.S. exports during the 2005-09 period averaged over $20,000 per year, and where exports of FTA competitors were somewhat significant—defined as accounting for more than a 5-percent total market share during our study period. For example, if the combined exports from China, Australia, and New Zealand accounted for less than 5 percent of total imports in an ASEAN country, that tariff line was not included in our analysis. Finally, tariff lines where the margin of preference, measured as the difference between the tariff that U.S. exports face and the tariff the FTA partners' exports will face after the FTAs have been fully implemented, is below 3 percent were also not considered to be vulnerable. Tables 4 and 5 display the trade amounts from the tariff lines that we believe would be the most vulnerable to increased competition as a result of the ASEAN-China and ASEAN-Oceania FTAs. The trade under these tariff lines was aggregated across commodity groupings (the number of tariff lines in each grouping is provided) for ease in analysis. The last three columns in the tables show the simple average margins of preference over these tariff lines as well as the minimum and maximum margin of preference within each commodity aggregate. Only the top 20 commodity groupings are provided in these tables, except in the case of New Zealand, where the identified tariff lines were contained within only 16 commodity groupings. In the six other countries found in tables 4 and 5, the top 20 commodity groupings accounted for at least 90 percent of all U.S. exports identified as most vulnerable. The first result that stands out is the importance of products in the category labeled "food preparations: composite mixtures." In all seven countries, this category is either first or second in terms of value of U.S. exports. This is a diverse grouping containing a number of tariff lines, but the bulk of U.S. exports are of products in the HS6 category 210690—food preparations not elsewhere specified or included.[11] The second notable result is the overall importance of processed products within these tables. In addition to food preparations, several other processed items account for large amounts of trade, including starches, miscellaneous agricultural products, bakery foods, and crude vegetable material. With certain exceptions (wheat to the Philippines, tobacco to Malaysia and China, corn to China, and cotton to China), few bulk commodities are found in these tables. High-value products such as fresh apples, grapes, certain dairy products, frozen potatoes, fats and oils, cocoa products, and prepared nuts and fruits are also important.

U.S. exports of products in the "food preparations: composite mixtures" category accounted for a total yearly average of about $190 million to the four ASEAN countries (see table 4). The average margins of preference for goods in this category range from 5.2 percent in Indonesia to 12.9 percent in Malaysia, with the maximum tariffs ranging from 7.5 percent in Indonesia to 30 percent in Thailand. The advantage that China, Australia, and New Zealand exporters will have over U.S. exporters may be fairly significant for some of these exports, so it should be no surprise that in the results of the model-based analysis, U.S. trade in processed foods declines by the largest amount, totaling $123.6 million per year in the ASEAN region.

Other important commodities exported to all four countries include fresh apples, fresh grapes, and frozen potatoes. U.S. exports of these products averaged between $8.6 million per year to Malaysia and $48.2 million to Indonesia, totaling over $100 million per year to the four ASEAN countries. The average margins of preference for these commodities range from 5 to 6 percent for most products in Indonesia to 30 percent or higher for some fruits and nuts in Thailand (see table 4). Model results show U.S. exports of fruits and vegetables to the ASEAN countries decreasing by over $50 million per year.

Table 4. Average margins of preference for Australia, New Zealand, and China in ASEAN countries - selected U.S. average exports, 2005-09

Product	United States	Australia	New Zealand	China	ASEAN	Rest of world	Total	No. of tariff lines	Margin of preference - ANZ			Margin of preference - China		
									Average	Mini-mum	Maxi-mum	Aver-age	Mini-mum	Maxi-mum
Indonesia				*$ thousands*										
Dairy: milk & cream,														
pwdr & cndnsd	83,721	81,217	128,010	79	91,268	74,900	459,195	7	5.7	5.0	10.0	5.7	5.0	10.0
Food prep:														
composite mixtures	36,983	8,797	15,689	12,347	41,255	82,646	197,716	11	5.2	5.0	7.5	5.2	5.0	7.5
Fruit (frsh): apples	23,946	1,226	2,145	71,405	563	2,340	101,625	1	5.0	5.0	5.0	5.0	5.0	5.0
Fruit (frsh): grapes	20,309	11,579	12	6,115	462	9,276	47,753	1	5.0	5.0	5.0	5.0	5.0	5.0
Dairy: other milk products	11,389	15,230	14,856	17	181	54,998	96,670	6	5.8	5.0	10.0	5.8	5.0	10.0
Starches (nonedible nes)	10,472	2,712	779	9,092	31,990	25,354	80,399	6	5.0	5.0	5.0	5.0	5.0	5.0
Dairy: cheese	6,373	14,425	12,122	18	1,468	2,317	36,723	5	5.0	5.0	5.0	5.0	5.0	5.0
Sweeteners: lactose														
& lactose syrup	5,447	451	2,561	103	84	6,425	15,071	4	5.0	5.0	5.0	5.0	5.0	5.0
Ag products: misc	4,740	3,165	56	4,641	7,210	21,009	40,820	6	5.8	5.0	10.0	5.8	5.0	10.0
Veg (prep): potatoes	4,502	235	513	489	1,045	2,548	9,332	3	5.0	5.0	5.0	5.0	5.0	5.0
Crude vegetable material	4,220	8		5,380	1,045	15,065	25,718	10	4.5	0.0	5.0	4.5	5.0	5.0
Veg (frzn): potatoes	3,969	167	898	136	463	4,781	10,414	1	5.0	5.0	5.0	5.0	5.0	5.0
Veg (frzn or prep):														
other	3,925	139	581	238	154	634	5,672	4	5.0	5.0	5.0	5.0	5.0	5.0
Feed: pet food	3,632	1,827	6	23	4,127	773	10,389	3	5.0	5.0	5.0	5.0	5.0	5.0
Meat (frsh or frzn):														

Product	United States	Australia	New Zealand	China	ASEAN	Rest of world	Total	No. of tariff lines	Margin of preference - ANZ Average	Margin of preference - ANZ Minimum	Margin of preference - ANZ Maximum	Margin of preference - China Average	Margin of preference - China Minimum	Margin of preference - China Maximum
edible offal	3,007	27,801	22,029		134	1,607	54,578	3	5.0	5.0	5.0	5.0	5.0	5.0
Crude animal material	2,438	146	298	1,355	282	226	4,746	4	5.4	5.0	6.7	5.4	5.0	6.7
Sweeteners: caramel														
& sugar nes	2,373	7,327	120	2,209	2,529	5,594	20,152	3	5.0	5.0	5.0	5.0	5.0	5.0
Nuts: almonds	2,198	184		5	10	23	2,421	1	5.0	5.0	5.0	5.0	5.0	5.0
Fruit (frsh): oranges	1,574	3,116		6,358	479	5,937	17,464	2	5.0	5.0	5.0	5.0	5.0	5.0
Veg (dried): other	1,535	9	57	2,503	265	371	4,740	2	5.0	5.0	5.0	5.0	5.0	5.0
Top 20	236,751	179,762	200,734	122,514	185,015	316,825	1,241,601	83						
Other	18,820	119,740	57,461	144,130	55,437	177,381	572,969	97						
Total	255,571	299,501	258,195	266,645	240,452	494,206	1,814,570	180						
Top 20 share	93%	60%	78%	46%	77%	64%	68%	46%						
Malaysia														
Food prep:														
composite mixtures	50,821	5,929	8,934	11,548	7,382	49,051	133,665	8	12.9	5.0	20.0	12.9	5.0	20.0
Tobacco (unmanufactured)	22,401	191		6,900	20,991	41,091	91,574	2	101.2	98.9	103.4	510.8	499.6	522.1
Cocoa products	6,223	6,350	2,050	3,101	1,959	27,829	47,512	5	15.0	15.0	15.0	15.0	15.0	15.0
Fruit (frsh): apples	4,362	247	1,909	13,402	29	12,231	32,179	1	5.0	5.0	5.0	5.0	5.0	5.0
Food prep: sauces	4,330	1,316	60	3,402	12,384	8,308	29,800	2	12.5	5.0	20.0	12.5	5.0	20.0
Fruit (frsh): grapes	3,920	2,573	9	1,191	25	4,351	12,069	1	5.0	5.0	5.0	5.0	5.0	5.0
Tobacco products	3,043	516		17,914	48,811	37,281	107,565	6	123.3	0.0	643.5	395.3	83.5	707.9
Veg (prep): potatoes	2,202	19	1	477	0	789	3,489	1	8.0	8.0	8.0	8.0	8.0	8.0
Fruit juice: mixtures	2,180	71	3,653	138	12	1,746	7,801	1	6.0	6.0	6.0	6.0	6.0	6.0
Fruit (dried): raisins	2,144	186	3	150	10	1,884	4,377	1	5.0	5.0	5.0	5.0	5.0	5.0
Beverages: wine	1,967	17,777	678	265	6	12,807	33,500	2	64.6	57.3	71.8	155.0	137.6	172.4
Sweeteners: glucose														
& glucose syrup	1,957			2,059	551	503	5,070	1	15.0	15.0	15.0	15.0	15.0	15.0

Table 4. (Continued)

Product	United States	Australia	New Zealand	China	ASEAN	Rest of world	Total	No. of tariff lines	Margin of preference - ANZ			Margin of preference - China		
									Aver-age	Mini-mum	Maxi-mum	Aver-age	Mini-mum	Maxi-mum
Grain prod: bakery foods	1,777	686	109	5,039	1,449	8,035	17,095	4	6.0	6.0	6.0	6.0	6.0	6.0
Dairy: cheese	1,763	14,190	12,242	12	1,188	3,438	32,832	3	6.7	5.0	10.0	6.7	5.0	10.0
Starches (nonedible nes)	1,232	160		9,405	0	2,113	12,910	3	5.7	5.0	6.0	5.7	5.0	6.0
Nuts: mixed or prepared	931			1,415	60	25	2,432	1	5.0	5.0	5.0	5.0	5.0	5.0
Beverages:														
nonalcoholic	858	215	8	384	681	428	2,574	3	20.0	20.0	20.0	20.0	20.0	20.0
Oil: peanut	850	632	53	7,019	6,393	2,902	17,850	2	15.0	15.0	15.0	15.0	15.0	15.0
Food prep: candy	850	401	5	192	7	664	2,120	3	5.0	5.0	5.0	5.0	5.0	5.0
Fruit (frsh): stone	737	8		208	434	1,703	3,090	1	5.0	5.0	5.0	5.0	5.0	5.0
Top 20	114,548	51,468	29,716	84,220	102,372	217,180	599,505	51						
Other	4,582	2,961	1,153	50,908	20,587	37,687	117,878	46						
Total	119,130	54,429	30,870	135,128	122,960	254,866	717,383	97						
Top 20 share	96%	95%	96%	62%	83%	85%	84%	53%						
Philippines														
Grain: wheat	347,884	22,603		22,844	215	104,995	498,541	4	4.5	3.0	7.0	4.5	3.0	7.0
Food prep:														
composite mixtures	23,340	2,407	4,979	8,292	33,937	29,931	102,885	20	6.7	3.0	15.0	6.7	3.0	15.0
Feed: pet food	12,130	2,927	41	1,661	8,420	10,248	35,428	4	14.0	5.0	35.0	2.5	0.0	5.0
Veg (frzn): potatoes	11,384	92	715	112	64	5,318	17,685	1	10.0	10.0	10.0	10.0	10.0	10.0
Meat (frzn): poultry	7,167	2,050	56	25	132	8,348	17,778	5	9.3	8.0	14.4	2.8	0.0	7.0
Fruit (frsh): grapes	6,334	683	16	104	2	1,093	8,232	1	7.0	7.0	7.0	7.0	7.0	7.0
Cocoa products	5,509	2,549	1,051	1,528	6,208	3,731	20,576	11	6.6	3.0	7.0	6.6	3.0	7.0

Product	United States	Australia	New Zealand	China	ASEAN	Rest of world	Total	No. of tariff lines	Margin of preference - ANZ			Margin of preference - China		
									Aver-age	Mini-mum	Maxi-mum	Aver-age	Mini-mum	Maxi-mum
Tobacco (unmanufactured)	5,049	186	173	21,331	14,083	114,282	155,105	4	7.0	7.0	7.0	7.0	7.0	7.0
Beverages: wine	4,682	2,212	179	43	396	5,493	13,006	6	6.7	5.0	7.0	6.7	5.0	7.0
Veg (prep):														
tomatoes	4,625	7	367	9,303	177	1,774	16,253	2	9.5	9.0	10.0	9.5	9.0	10.0
Sweeteners: glucose														
& glucose syrup	4,197	6	1	9,685	2,312	3,015	19,216	4	3.0	3.0	3.0	3.0	3.0	3.0
Veg (dried): beans, peas, & lentils	4,190	506	11	992	2,611	2,988	11,296	6	4.2	3.0	10.0	4.2	3.0	10.0
Starches (nonedible nes)	2,952	55	62	1,761	4,578	5,380	14,788	4	3.0	3.0	3.0	3.0	3.0	3.0
Meat (frzn): beef	2,916	11,357	4,222	140	120	113,641	132,396	2	10.0	10.0	10.0	10.0	10.0	10.0
Dairy: other milk products	2,470	8,743	23,507	176	2,513	6,607	44,015	4	4.0	3.0	7.0	4.0	3.0	7.0
Grain: corn	2,011	1,540		774	30	3,877	8,233	2	11.2	7.0	15.3	7.8	7.0	8.5
Sweeteners: carmel														
& sugar nes	1,910	127		5,319	1,136	4,825	13,317	4	3.0	3.0	3.0	3.0	3.0	3.0
Dairy: cheese	1,872	9,697	21,371	7	469	2,964	36,378	5	5.4	3.0	7.0	5.4	3.0	7.0
Crude vegetable material	1,782	37	18	3,166	597	6,097	11,696	5	3.8	3.0	7.0	3.8	3.0	7.0
Crude animal material	1,619	601	593	1	44	584	3,441	3	3.0	3.0	3.0	3.0	3.0	3.0
Top 20	454,022	68,386	57,364	87,263	78,044	435,190	1,180,268	97						
Other	22,319	23,674	22,921	70,505	70,304	80,642	290,36	128						
Total	476,341	92,059	80,285	157,768	148,347	515,832	1,470,632	225						
Top 20 share	95%	74%	71%	55%	53%	84%	80%	43%						
Thailand														

Table 4. (Continued)

Product	United States	Australia	New Zealand	China	ASEAN	Rest of world	Total	No. of tariff lines	Margin of preference - ANZ			Margin of preference - China		
									Aver-age	Mini-mum	Maxi-mum	Aver-age	Mini-mum	Maxi-mum
Food prep:														
composite mixtures	76,679	11,940	5,617	12,073	60,634	84,641	251,584	18	7.8	5.0	30.0	7.8	5.0	30.0
Feed: pet food	66,502	11,403	46	14,952	10,647	78,582	182,132	8	9.0	9.0	9.0	4.0	4.0	4.0
Skins & hides:														
bovine	54,987	36,403	3,443	127	7,509	56,669	159,139	5	5.0	5.0	5.0	5.0	5.0	5.0
Dairy: other milk products	31,988	39,030	75,208	1,575	356	44,708	192,865	5	11.3	5.0	30.0	2.3	0.0	11.5
Fruit (frsh): apples	13,807	10,370	23,542	286	147	35,846	83,997	9	20.3	5.0	30.0	20.3	5.0	30.0
Feed: waste & residues nes	11,923			3,271	135	6,869	22,198	4	0.0	0.0	0.0	30.0	30.0	30.0
Fruit (frsh): grapes	11,063	92	4,911	54,340	116	4,958	75,480	1	12.3	12.3	12.3	12.3	12.3	12.3
Veg (frzn): potatoes	10,202			934	14	2,151	13,301	3	6.3	5.0	9.0	6.3	5.0	9.0
Nuts & fruit (dried & frsh) nes	10,113	7,456		14,965	121	4,079	36,735	1	30.0	30.0	30.0	30.0	30.0	30.0
Starches (nonedible nes)	10,106	59	2,213	525	33	3,197	16,133	1	30.0	30.0	30.0	30.0	30.0	30.0
Crude vegetable material	8,304	813	550	7,973	249	15,160	33,048	10	13.8	5.0	27.0	13.8	5.0	27.0
Nuts: almonds	8,206	114	1,022	8,526	6,293	1,597	25,759	8	38.8	30.0	40.0	34.6	23.3	40.0
Live poultry	5,759	321	6	168	0	46	6,300	2	10.1	10.0	10.3	10.1	10.0	10.3
Food prep:														
margarine	4,216	680	1,259	6,742	8,001	18,115	39,014	7	12.1	0.0	30.0	16.3	5.0	30.0
Fruit (prep): stone	2,720	213			0	225	3,158	1	15.0	15.0	15.0	15.0	15.0	15.0
Cocoa products	2,558	867	112	126	5,253	1,468	10,384	3	28.5	25.4	30.0	28.5	25.4	30.0
Tea extracts	2,483	11		5,634	147	16,055	24,331	3	30.0	30.0	30.0	30.0	30.0	30.0

Product	United States	Australia	New Zealand	China	ASEAN	Rest of world	Total	No. of tariff lines	Margin of preference - ANZ			Margin of preference - China		
									Aver-age	Mini-mum	Maxi-mum	Aver-age	Mini-mum	Maxi-mum
Nuts & fruit (prepared) nes	2,480	2,251	632	1,685	3,668	8,300	19,016	4	10.0	10.0	10.0	10.0	10.0	10.0
Fruit juice:														
grapefruit	2,462	1	0	1,446	529	2,107	6,545	3	30.0	30.0	30.0	30.0	30.0	30.0
Food prep: sauces	2,427	399	363	9,153	362		15,075	8	30.0	30.0	30.0	27.5	25.0	30.0
Top 20	338,984	122,423	118,924	144,502	104,213	387,144	1,216,191	104						
Other	36,151	49,721	21,051	130,011	143,448	233,341	613,723	165						
Total	375,135	172,144	139,976	274,514	247,661	620,486	1,829,914	269						
Top 20 share	90%	71%	85%	53%	42%	62%	66%	39%						

ASEAN = Association of Southeast Asian Nations. ANZ = Australia/New Zealand. nes = not elsewhere specified.

Source: USDA, Economic Research Service calculations using 2005-09 trade data in the Global Trade Atlas and tariff data in ERS databases.

Table 5. Average margins of preference for ASEAN countries in China, Australia, and New Zealand – selected U.S. average exports, 2005-09

Product	United States	ASEAN	Rest of world	Total	No. of tariff lines	Margin of preference - ASEAN[1]		
						Average	Minimum	Maximum
China		*$ thousands*						
Food prep: composite mixtures	96,808	33,187	251,590	381,585	3	16.7	10.0	20.0
Starches (nonedible nes)	19,882	60,086	40,263	120,230	2	16.0	12.0	20.0
Ag products: misc	16,153	276,749	110,592	403,495	8	14.3	10.0	16.0
Oil: soybean	10,670	1,422	7,746	19,838	1	10.9	10.9	10.9
Crude vegetable material	8,791	16,877	31,840	57,508	9	13.2	6.0	20.0
Cocoa butter and paste	8,350	4,438	13,032	25,820	1	10.0	10.0	10.0
Fats & oils: animal & veg nes	8,071	16,662	32,907	57,640	2	15.0	10.0	20.0
Essential oils	6,249	9,764	21,981	37,993	3	15.0	15.0	15.0
Food prep: sauces	6,164	25,518	29,122	60,804	1	20.0	20.0	20.0
Grain: corn	4,873	8,786	58,853	72,512	1	21.0	21.0	21.0
Grain prod: bakery foods	3,844	7,387	31,412	42,643	4	7.5	0.0	10.0
Fiber: cotton (carded)	3,712	5,157	185	9,053	1	15.0	15.0	15.0
Grain prod: breakfast cereal	3,509	9,519	62,845	75,872	5	19.0	15.0	25.0
Tobacco (unmanufactured)	2,842	3,482	7,229	13,553	2	27.5	25.0	30.0
Food prep: candy	2,801	2,601	5,082	10,484	1	5.0	5.0	5.0
Nuts & fruit (prepared) nes	2,564	7,937	26,747	37,248	3	17.3	10.0	30.0
Veg (prep): other	2,332	1,870	2,162	6,365	2	15.0	15.0	15.0
Fats & oils: vegetable	2,236	17,722	3,768	23,725	2	12.5	10.0	15.0
Crude animal material	2,041	1,372	1,561	4,974	5	21.0	10.0	25.0
Food prep: pasta (stuffed)	1,947	170,192	7,506	179,645	2	22.5	20.0	25.0
Top 20	213,840	680,729	746,421	1,640,989	58			
Other	22,152	865,847	312,826	1,200,826	66			
Total	235,992	1,546,576	1,059,247	2,841,815	124			
Product	United	ASEAN	Rest of	Total	No. of	Margin of preference - ASEAN[1]		

	States		world		tariff lines	Average	Minimum	Maximum
Top 20 share	91%	44%	70%	58%	47%			
Australia								
Food prep: composite mixtures	74,379	42,121	570,999	687,499	2	4.5	4	5
Grain prod: bakery foods	10,662	33,321	147,794	191,777	3	5	5	5
Nuts & fruit (prepared) nes	7,764	7,598	103,864	119,226	2	5	5	5
Fruit juice: mixtures	5,406	5,109	16,650	27,165	4	5	5	5
Beverages: distilled spirits nes	4,982	8,531	16,008	29,521	1	5	5	5
Veg (prep): other	4,412	1,345	18,633	24,390	1	5	5	5
Grain prod: breakfast cereal	1,369	2,053	6,963	10,385	1	5	5	5
Veg (frzn): other	1,213	8,290	34,345	43,847	5	5	5	5
Sweeteners: carmel & sugar nes	1,153	4,098	22,318	27,568	2	4.5	4	5
Nuts & fruit (dried & frsh) nes	1,054	1,267	11,631	13,952	1	5	5	5
Food prep: pasta (stuffed)	1,052	3,034	46,913	51,000	1	5	5	5
Oil: cottonseed	1,014	819	4,512	6,345	1	5	5	5
Food prep: margarine	989	1,106	5,501	7,596	2	5	5	5
Oil: soybean	923	9,749	5,863	16,535	1	5	5	5
Oil: linseed	827	7,280	23,407	31,513	1	5	5	5
Ag products: misc	640	4,314	2,987	7,941	1	5	5	5
Nuts: mixed or prepared	529	22,295	7,388	30,212	2	5	5	5
Food prep: candy	313	23,113	47,349	70,775	1	5	5	5
Veg (dried & frsh): roots & tubers	199	8,580	5,326	14,105	1	5	5	5
Food prep: soup	198	240	1,142	1,580	1	5	5	5
Top 20	119,078	194,262	1,099,593	1,412,932	34			
Other	570	4,667	9,439	14,676	6			
Total	119,648	198,928	1,109,032	1,427,608	40			
Top 20 share	99.5%	98%	99%	99%	85%			
New Zealand								
Food prep: composite mixtures	28,591	12,208	150,405	191,204	3	6.8	6.5	7.0

Table 5. (Continued)

Product	United States	ASEAN	Rest of world	Total	No. of tariff lines	Margin of preference - ASEAN[1]		
						Average	Minimum	Maximum
Feed: pet food	15,073	3,840	25,234	44,147	2	6.8	6.5	7.0
Food prep: sauces	2,711	4,870	30,418	37,999	1	6.5	6.5	6.5
Nuts & fruit (prepared) nes	761	759	6,075	7,594	1	7.0	7.0	7.0
Nuts & fruit (dried & frsh) nes	411	208	1,754	2,373	1	5.0	5.0	5.0
Sweeteners: carmel & sugar nes	393	60	394	847	1	5.0	5.0	5.0
Veg (frzn): other	375	145	207	726	1	7.0	7.0	7.0
Beverages: nonalcoholic	260	524	6,223	7,007	2	5.8	5.0	6.5
Cocoa products	190	3,127	13,515	16,832	1	6.5	6.5	6.5
Fats & oils: vegetable	142	4,515	986	5,642	1	5.0	5.0	5.0
Dairy: milk & cream, pwdr & cndnsd	85	189	2,822	3,095	1	5.0	5.0	5.0
Cocoa powder	76	220	1,623	1,919	1	6.5	6.5	6.5
Fruit (prep): composite mixtures	68	744	5,345	6,157	1	6.5	6.5	6.5
Veg (frzn or prep): other	41	17	116	175	1	6.5	6.5	6.5
Grain prod: flour (wheat)	29	828	4,958	5,815	1	6.0	6.0	6.0
Grain prod: flour (nonwheat)	26	549	587	1,162	1	5	5	5
Total	49,230	32,803	250,662	332,694	20			
nes = not elsewhere specified.								

[1]The free trade agreement (FTA) between the United States and Australia brought most bilateral tariffs to zero. Margins of preference for Australia are the pre-existing Australian tariffs facing ASEAN (Association of Southeast Asian Nations), which disappear as the FTA with ASEAN is implemented.

Source: USDA, Economic Research Service calculations using 2005-09 trade data in the Global Trade Atlas and tariff data in ERS databases.

Products in a number of important tariff lines (in terms of export value) identified as vulnerable are primarily exported by the United States to only one or two countries, including wheat and frozen poultry to the Philippines; powdered and condensed milk to Indonesia; pet food, hides and skins, and dairy products to Thailand; and unmanufactured tobacco and cocoa products to Malaysia. Among these products, model results show that U.S. poultry exports to the Philippines are particularly vulnerable, with projected losses of almost $40 million per year. U.S. wheat exports to the Philippines averaged almost $350 million per year, representing the largest traded item in the list. The modeling analysis projected losses of only $20 million in U.S. wheat exports to the Philippines, largely because the margin of preference is fairly low, averaging 4.5 percent, and the United States is by far the dominant supplier. Of the Philippines' total wheat imports, the United States had an average market share of 70 percent versus only 5 percent each for Australia and China, and the majority of these exports entered at an MFN applied rate of only 3 percent, so the vulnerability of U.S. wheat exports is borderline according to our criteria. U.S. tobacco and tobacco product exports to Malaysia appear vulnerable given the rather large margins of preference provided by the FTAs. As a large competing exporter in both these markets, China could capture market share from the United States. These products would be included in the GTAP model category "Other agriculture," where U.S. exports are projected to drop by $6.2 million per year.

At a total value of $235 million per year, the amount of U.S. exports to China identified as vulnerable is small relative to total U.S. exports to China (see table 5). As stated earlier, the vast majority of U.S. exports to China do not compete directly with exports from ASEAN countries; for most U.S. products that faced some competition, the amount exported by ASEAN countries was extremely low. In addition, many tariffs in HS Chapters 1-8 were reduced to zero under the Early Harvest Program in 2004.

As in some of the ASEAN countries, the largest vulnerable category of U.S. exports in China was "food preparations: composite mixtures" followed by starches (HS Chapter 35), miscellaneous agricultural products (mannitol, sorbitol, glycerol, stearic and oleic acid, etc.), and soybean oil. These four categories accounted for over 60 percent of all identified vulnerable U.S. exports. The average margins of preference for ASEAN exporters tend to be higher, averaging between 11 and 17 percent for these four commodity groupings, partly because China tends to apply tariffs at or near their bound levels.

In Australia, the category "food preparations: composite mixtures" accounted for $74 million per year—over 60 percent of the vulnerable products total— in U.S. exports. Baked goods (e.g., mixes and dough, bread, pastries) were the next highest category. The margins of preference were between 4 and 5 percent across the board for Australia. As stated earlier, the advantage that U.S. exporters already receive over ASEAN exporters under the U.S.- Australia FTA will disappear as a result of the ASEAN-Australia FTA, as will the margins of preference listed in table 5 that favor U.S. exporters. Finally, the amount of U.S. exports to New Zealand identified as vulnerable is very small, although like the product mix exported to the other countries, it tends to consist mainly of processed products.

THE PENDING U.S. TAs WITH KOREA, COLOMBIA, AND PANAMA

The United States signed successive TAs with Colombia, Panama, and Korea between November 2006 and June 2007. Each agreement, however, still awaits U.S. congressional approval before it can be implemented. All three pending agreements are comprehensive TAs that contain market access provisions of interest to U.S. agriculture. In addition to eventually eliminating tariffs and quotas on most agricultural goods, each agreement has sought to address other nontariff barriers, particularly SPS measures.

As with most FTAs, the agricultural negotiations addressed how to protect producers of imported sensitive commodities. For most commodities, negotiators agreed on long implementation periods, which in some cases delayed the initial tariff cut for several years (app. 2, table 3). In the case of the KORUS, 21 percent of U.S. agricultural tariff lines are already free of duty, compared with only 2 percent for Korea. Of the more than 1,810 U.S. and 1,550 Korean tariff lines, approximately 58 percent of U.S. tariff lines and approximately 38 percent of Korean tariff lines would be free of duty or would become so immediately upon entry into force of the TA. One hundred percent of U.S. tariff lines and 98 percent of Korean tariff lines would have free rates of duty by the end of the implementation period. In the case of the CTPA, 68 percent of U.S. agricultural tariff lines and 78 percent of Colombian agricultural tariff lines are already free of duty or will become so immediately upon implementation of the CTPA. While 21 percent of U.S. tariff lines are already free of duty, none of Colombia's agricultural tariff lines are categorized as already free of duty. Because of this tariff asymmetry, the immediate effects of the TA will be a relatively large improvement in U.S. access to the Colombian market. In the case of the PTPA, 89 percent of U.S. agricultural lines and 68 percent of Panamanian agricultural lines are already free of duty or would become so immediately upon implementation of the TA. U.S. tariff commitments would largely make permanent the duty-free provisions that Colombia receives under the Andean Trade Promotion Act (ATPA) and that Panama receives under the Caribbean Basin Economic Recovery Act (CBERA). In the cases of both the CTPA and the PTPA, and as opposed to KORUS, the United States excluded 47 tariff lines from the agreement. These include over-quota tariffs on items such as sugar and sugar-containing products. In many cases, the agreements include new, country-specific TRQs to allow some duty-free treatment during the transition period. In addition, the agreements allow for the imposition of safeguards or temporary higher tariffs in the case of import surges. For a few of the most sensitive commodities, import TRQs were created that allow for increased market access over time, but the tariffs on imports in excess of these quotas would not be cut—protection for these commodities would remain at the MFN level. Finally, in the most extreme example, the United States agreed to Korea's request that rice be completely excluded from their TA.

THE U.S.-KOREA TRADE AGREEMENT (KORUS)

Structure of Agricultural Trade

Korea, a longstanding major market for U.S. agricultural exports, was the fifth largest country market for U.S. agriculture in 2007-09. The United States is the largest supplier of Korea's agricultural imports, with a share over 25 percent in recent years. U.S. imports from Korea averaged $290 million during 2007-09, placing Korea 41st as a supplier of agricultural commodities to the United States. Leading U.S. imports from Korea were specialty food products, ramen noodles, cigarettes, and fresh pears and quinces. The United States runs a positive agricultural trade balance with Korea, averaging over $4 billion during 2007-09 (table 6). U.S. agricultural exports to Korea can be divided into supplies that are inputs for Korean industries and products that compete with the outputs of Korean industries for consumer expenditures. Some of the inputs include wheat, corn, soybeans, cotton, and hides used in processing. These input commodities usually are imported with little or no tariff (see box,

"Korean TRQs"). This is because (1) they do not displace domestic Korean production, and (2) the industries that use them need low-cost inputs to compete in the Korean and global marketplaces. On the other hand, products that compete with domestic Korean production are often assessed a tariff that helps the Korean producer maintain higher prices.[12] In the last decade, U.S. agricultural exports to Korea have typically been split between the two categories, with about half of the exports in 2009 filling the input role and paying almost no tariff (fig. 2).

Table 6. Composition of U.S. agricultural trade with Korea, 2007-09 averages

Product	Main U.S. exports		Product	Main U.S. imports	
	Value	Share of total		Value	Share of total
	$ millions	*Percent*		*$ millions*	*Percent*
Corn	1,369.9	31.4	Food preparations	53.7	18.5
Wheat	375.5	8.6	Pasta products	34.8	12.0
Cattle hides	279.7	6.4	Nonalcoholic beverages	33.2	11.5
Soybeans	207.5	4.8	Tobacco products	29.2	10.1
Pork: fresh, chilled, frozen	204.8	4.7	Fresh pears and quinces	23.0	7.9
Beef: fresh, chilled, frozen	203.5	4.7	Baked products and pastries	21.2	7.3
Food preparations	174.0	4.0	Nuts and fruit, prepared	14.8	5.1
Hay and other forage products	168.9	3.9	Locust beans, seaweeds and other algae	9.3	3.2
Cotton	111.1	2.5	Ethyl alcohol	8.6	3.0
Nuts	93.6	2.1	Vegetable saps and extracts	6.0	2.1
Subtotal, top 10	3,188.5	73.0	Subtotal, top 10	233.8	80.7
All other agricultural products	1,179.3	27.0	All other agricultural products	55.9	19.3
Total	4,367.8	100.0	Total	289.6	100.0

Source: USDA, Economic Research Service using U.S. International Trade Commission's Dataweb.

Korean TRQs

Korea currently makes widespread use of tariff-rate quotas (TRQs) for agricultural products. TRQs for corn, soybeans, and soymeal are of interest to the United States. These TRQs provide protection for a certain group of Korean farmers or manufacturers.

The TRQs have very low within-quota tariff levels and very high over-quota levels (see table). For major commodities, even the within-quota tariff levels are sometimes waived. For example, the over-quota tariff for corn for feeding is 328 percent. The within-quota tariff is 3 percent. However, the actual applied tariff is 0. Korean farmers grow limited quantities of corn and soybeans. If industries in Korea do not purchase the farmers' output at the high prices necessitated by high costs of production, the Korean Government can reduce the TRQ quantities or raise the in-quota tariffs. This has not occurred in the past.

Korea also uses the TRQ method to lower tariffs. For commodities such as soymeal for which there is no WTO-committed TRQ, the Korean Government has chosen to open new voluntary TRQs that offer a lower tariff rate to a limited volume of imports. In the case of soymeal, the TRQ quantity far exceeds the maximum import level of the past. Using this method, Korea has the option of revising tariffs periodically. For instance, a low tariff on a large commodity flow can be reinstituted to raise a substantial amount of Government revenue.

Selected Korean tariff rate quotas (TRQ)

				TRQ quantity	
	Overquota	In-quota, base	In-quota, adjusted	Base	Voluntary 2010
		Tariff, in percent		Metric tons	
Corn for feeding	328	3	0	6,102,100	9,000,000
Corn for starch	328	3	1		1,850,000
Soybeans for crushing1	487	3	0	846,365	1,200,000
Soybeans for other uses1	487	5	5	185,787	266,800
Soymeal for feed	1.8		1	unlimited	2,700,000
TRQ = tariff-rate quota.					

[1]The tariff for soybeans is 487 percent or 956 won/kg, whichever is greater.

Sources: USDA, Economic Research Service using Tariff Schedules of Korea, 2006; USDA, Foreign Agricultural Service reports KS1002 and KS 1013.

In KORUS, U.S. exporters have little to gain from the elimination of very low tariffs on the input commodities. Rather, U.S. interests are more focused on commodities that have higher tariffs. These commodities tend to compete with commodities produced in Korea.

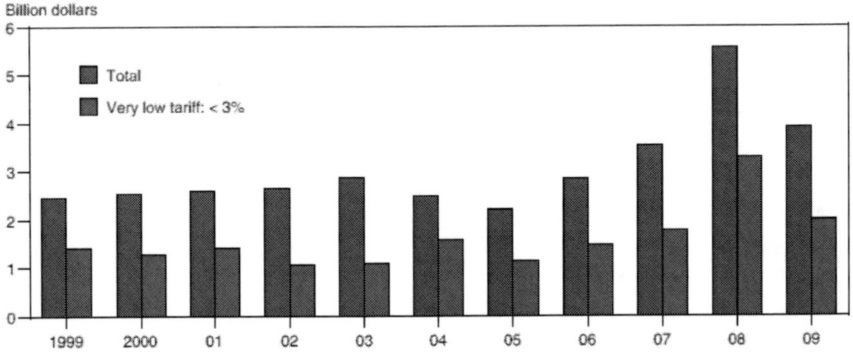

Note: Very low tariff includes wheat, corn, soybeans, cotton, and hides.
Source: USDA, Economic Research Service using USDA's Foreign Agricultural Trade of the United States database.

Figure 2. U.S. agricultural exports to Korea.

Agricultural Provisions of KORUS

The largest output of Korean agriculture, rice, is not subject to the proposed FTA. For 16 other tariff lines, trade will not be opened to unlimited quantities from the United States at zero tariffs, but TRQs will be set up specifically for limited imports from the United States. These commodities include oranges imported in September-February, powdered and evaporated milk, honey, fresh potatoes not for chipping, and soybeans for food manufacture and sprouting. Initially small, the TRQs will be raised by 3 percent per year, indefinitely.

For all other products, at some point Korea promises to allow all imports from the United States to enter with a zero tariff. The timeframe varies according to the product and can be as long as 17 years from when the TA enters into force. The products from which the United States could gain the most from KORUS include those where tariffs are substantial, competition with Korean producers and foreign exporters is strong, and/or Korean demand responds strongly to lower prices. Exports from the United States that meet all three criteria are likely to be those that grow the most as the TA is implemented. When tariffs on U.S. products are reduced and eventually eliminated, the price of U.S. products in the Korean market should fall. At lower prices, U.S. products compete more effectively against domestic Korean and other imported products. Lower prices may also lead to increases in purchases of specific products by Korean consumers. Tariff reductions under the TA will allow U.S. products to be more competitive with those of countries currently benefiting from, or negotiating, reduced tariffs with Korea. Chile already has an FTA with Korea and has seen its pork exports to Korea grow strongly as tariffs facing Chilean pork have declined. The EU has negotiated an FTA with Korea, but it is not yet ratified or implemented. If the Korea-EU FTA takes effect, EU exports will have a tariff margin of preference over exports from the United States and other countries.

Potential Impact on U.S. Agricultural Exports

Animal Products

Model results show that growth in U.S. beef exports to Korea in response to tariff reductions will be the single largest commodity change, with over $550 million per year in new trade, or 29 percent of total U.S. agricultural trade growth (table 7). Beginning in the first year of implementation, tariffs facing U.S. beef would be reduced by about 2.7 percent per year, until they reach zero 15 years after implementation. It is important to note that trade liberalization in this analysis is interpreted as instantaneous removal or reduction of all tariffs. In reality, the pace of export growth may be affected over time by a safeguard mechanism in the agreement to address import surges. If triggered, this safeguard would impose a higher tariff on imports above the trigger level. The trigger level increases each year, and the tariffs imposed on trade above the trigger level decrease over time. It is expected that U.S. beef will become steadily more competitive with beef originating from Korea, Australia, and New Zealand.[13] U.S. beef has proven popular in Korea in the past and accounted for about 10 percent of Korea's beef market in 2007-09 (table 8). The ability of U.S. companies to source the particular cuts that Korean companies find most profitable is unparalleled because of the following factors:

- The U.S. beef herd and slaughter numbers are the second largest in the world; more slaughtered cattle can provide more of the specific cuts wanted in Korea.
- Only countries completely free of foot-and-mouth disease can ship uncooked beef and pork to Korea; this prevents much of Asia, South America, and Europe from shipping to Korea.

- U.S. beef is predominantly grainfed, in contrast to the largely grassfed cattle herds of Oceania. Korean consumers have shown a preference for grainfed beef.
- Cuts desired by Korean companies are often those that sell at a relatively low price in the United States because of taste and culinary differences between the two countries.

Other U.S. meat exports (mainly pork) to Korea are estimated to increase substantially due to lower prices and consumer preferences for the cuts that can be sourced profitably from the United States. Pork bellies and bone-in chicken legs, for example, are more valuable in Korea than in the United States because of differing tastes and cooking techniques. Pork and poultry exports from the United States are expected to rise by over $275 million per year, representing 14 percent of total U.S. agricultural export growth stemming from full KORUS implementation (see table 7). Korean tariffs on frozen U.S. pork will be zero as of January 1, 2016, if KORUS is implemented before then. Korean tariffs on imports of boneless chilled pork, frozen chicken legs, and frozen chicken offal from the United States will decrease to zero 10 years after implementation. In the case of chilled pork cuts, a safeguard mechanism may slow the growth of Korean imports by temporarily raising tariffs if annual trigger levels are exceeded. The increasing margins of preference accruing to U.S. exports of these products will help them compete with exports from the EU, Canada, and Chile (which already enjoys lower tariffs) and may also enhance U.S. competitiveness with Korean pork and poultry meat.[14] Growth in exports of U.S. dairy products to Korea is projected to be 145 percent, or more than $90 million per year (see table 7). Although Korean tariffs on milk powders from the United States in general are not reduced, the United States may gain from a small country-specific TRQ on powdered and evaporated milk that is duty free. In the case of cheese, a TRQ for Korean imports from the United States will grow each year, with zero duty within the TRQ. However, after 15 years, all U.S. exports become duty free (10 years, in the case of cheddar cheese). For butter and food whey, U.S.-specific TRQs provide duty-free access in addition to the existing WTO TRQs, and, after 10 years, all U.S. exports of these products to Korea become duty free. Korea's dairy industry is high cost relative to the U.S. industry, and the tariff advantages that the United States will receive will make its products more competitive against those of Oceania and the EU as well.

Table 7. Projected effect on U.S. exports to Korea due to KORUS

	Tariff average	Base ($ millions)	Change ($ millions)	Percent change
Rice	450.0	48	-1	-2.8
Wheat	2.2	299	30	10.0
Other grains	0.0	1,237	-12	-1.0
Fruits and vegetables	51.5	281	133	47.3
Oilseeds	5.0	357	50	13.9
Cotton	1.0	116	14	12.3
Beef	37.3	701	563	80.3
Poultry and pork	24.9	291	276	94.9
Other livestock products	4.2	316	49	15.4
Oilseed products	6.8	90	34	37.3
Dairy products	44.0	64	93	145.9
Processed food and fish	18.4	926	404	43.7
Other agricultural products	46.6	237	301	127.0
Total agriculture		4,962	1,933	38.9

KORUS = U.S.-Korea Trade Agreement.

Source: USDA, Economic Research Service results of Global Trade Analysis Project modeling exercise for this study; base year is 2014.

Table 8. Korea's animal product imports from the United States

	Tariff	Korean imports from U.S.	U.S. share of:[1]		Competitors	Phase-in
			Imports	Market		
	Percent	*$ millions*	*Percent*			*Years*
Chilled and frozen beef	40	171	16	9	Korea, Australia, New Zealand	15
Chilled and frozen pork	22.5,25[2]	206	29	9	Korea, EU, Canada, Chile	10[3]
Frozen chicken meat and offal	20	38	51	4	Korea, Brazil	10, 12[2]
Edible offal of cattle and swine	18	12	13	NA	Australia, New Zealand, EU	15[3]
Prepared/preserved meat and offal	27,30,72[2]	13	10	NA	Korea, China, Thailand, EU	15
Cheese	36	42	19	13	New Zealand, Australia, EU	10,12,15[2]

NA = not available.

[1] Trade and market data are the average for 2007-09.

[2] Subcategories have different tariffs or phase-in periods.

[3] Some subcategories enjoy a zero tariff as of 1/1/2016. Others are phased in from the first implementation year.

Sources: USDA, Economic Research Service using Tariff Schedules of Korea; USDA's Production, Supply, and Distribution database; and official import data of Korea.

Growth in exports of animal products to Korea will contribute just over 50 percent of the projected total U.S. agricultural export gains from the TA. Some of this growth will come from the existing exports of competing countries, and some will come from new Korean demand stimulated by lower prices. Because market share will likely be taken from Korean livestock and poultry industries, production of animal products in Korea is expected to fall, resulting in less need for feedstuffs such as corn and soymeal. Imports of those products are expected to decrease, including from the United States. The expected decrease, however, is only 1 percent per year.

Other Products

The other half of U.S. agriculture's export gains from full KORUS implementation is projected to come from exports of processed foods and fish products, other agricultural products, fruits and vegetables, oilseeds and oilseed products, wheat, and cotton.

Processed foods and fish exports may account for about 20 percent of the gains to U.S. agricultural exports to Korea. Processed foods include a large number of trade categories, and over $130 million of this trade is characterized simply as "other processed products." Thus, a full description of the segment is difficult. Large, identifiable subcategories include processed fruits and vegetables, snack foods, and fruit juices (app. 2, table 2). Tariffs vary widely, from relatively low levels on chocolates to extremely high levels on some Korean specialty products. Korean firms manufacture many processed products, but global markets can supply even more types. In this highly competitive environment, duty-free access should benefit U.S. exporters.

Korea is a major fish-consuming and fish-harvesting country. U.S. fish product exports to Korea, centered on roe and surimi (fish paste) from Alaskan pollock, averaged about $300 million in 2007-09. Model results project an increase of over 40 percent in U.S. exports of processed foods and fish products if KORUS is fully implemented (see table 7).

"Other agricultural products" is a residual category with many parts. It includes beverages, tobacco, essential oils, sugar, and nursery products (app. 2, table 2). U.S. exports of wine, tobacco products, waters, and other branded products to Korea could benefit from tariff reduction, especially in the face of competition from the EU and Oceania. Model results project an increase of over 100 percent in this category.

U.S. fruit and vegetable exports to Korea are projected to grow by $133 million per year as a result of KORUS (see table 7). U.S. exports, averaged over 2007-09, were dominated by $83 million in orange shipments and $88 million in nut exports (table 9). Oranges are not fully liberalized in the TA. The 50-percent tariff is retained in the September-February period, but a small TRQ with zero duty is set up for imports in that period from the United States. The TRQ grows by 3 percent in perpetuity. For the March-August period, duties are reduced until they reach zero at the beginning of the seventh year after implementation. U.S. exports of nuts and other fruits would benefit from relatively early tariff reductions.

In sum, model results project a gain of over $1.9 billion per year in U.S. exports to Korea upon full TA implementation (see table 7). Of this increase, 95 percent will occur in high-value food items such as livestock products, processed products, and fruits. Bulk commodities, such as wheat, corn, soybeans, and cotton, already face low tariffs and will be minimally affected by the TA. The increase in U.S. exports to Korea represents 39 percent growth over base levels. Earlier model results made by the USITC projected gains of $1.9 billion to $3.8 billion (USITC, 2007a).[15]

Table 9. U.S. fruit, vegetable, and nut exports to Korea

	U.S. exports	Tariff[2]	Phase-in
	$ millions	*Percent*	*Years*
Fresh fruits	138		
Oranges	83	50	0
Cherries	26	24	
Other	29		
Fresh vegetables	9	8-304	0-15[3]
Frozen fruits	1	30	5-15
Frozen vegetables	2	27, 30	0-15
Nuts	88		
Shelled walnuts	41	30	6
Shelled almonds	37	8	0
Others	9		

[1] Trade data are averages for 2007-09.

[2] Frozen vegetable tariffs are either 27 or 30 percent.

[3] Tariffs on potatoes, not for chipping or seed, are not cut in the agreement.

Sources: USDA, Economic Research Service calculations using Tariff Schedules of Korea and USDA's BICO (bulk, intermediate, and consumer) database.

Total U.S. imports of agricultural products from Korea are estimated to increase about $60 million per year (table 10). Growth in imports of agricultural products from Korea would primarily be in processed products, which currently face U.S. tariffs of about 6 percent. Ethnic foods, such as biscuits, savory snack foods, ramen noodles, and seaweed products, would account for the bulk of the increase.

Table 10. Projected effect on U.S. imports from Korea due to KORUS

	Tariff average	Base	Change	Percent change
		----*$ millions*----		
Rice	7.0	2.8	1.5	53.8
Wheat	0.0	0.0	0.0	0.0
Other grains	0.0	0.1	0.0	4.5
Fruits and vegetables	1.0	41.4	0.6	1.5
Oilseeds	10.1	0.4	0.2	52.4
Cotton	0.0	0.1	0.0	0.0
Beef	0.0	0.6	0.0	2.6
Poultry and pork	2.5	1.3	0.2	14.6
Other livestock products	0.2	3.2	0.1	2.8
Oilseed products	4.1	0.8	0.6	65.8
Dairy products	48.1	4.8	11.0	228.5
Processed foods	5.5	184.3	28.2	15.3
Beverages and tobacco products	6.2	100.9	17.1	16.9
Total agriculture		340.7	59.4	17.4
KORUS = U.S.-Korea Trade Agreement.				

Source: USDA, Economic Research Service results of Global Trade Analysis Project modeling exercise for this study; base year is 2014.

THE U.S-COLOMBIA TRADE PROMOTION AGREEMENT (CTPA)

Structure of Agricultural Trade

Colombia was the second largest South American market for U.S. farm products in 2007-09 and the 21st most important market for U.S. agriculture overall. U.S. shipments of corn, wheat, soybeans, cotton, and soybean meal topped the list, accounting for over three-quarters of total exports (table 11). During 2007-09, U.S. products accounted for 39 percent of Colombia's $3.5 billion annual agricultural import market. Other major exporters to Colombia were Argentina, Brazil, Canada, Chile, the EU, and members of the Andean Common Market (Bolivia, Ecuador, and Peru).

Table 11. Composition of U.S. agricultural trade with Colombia, 2007-09 averages

Product	Main U.S. exports		Product	Main U.S. imports	
	Value	Share of total		Value	Share of total
	$ millions	*Percent*		*$ millions*	*Percent*
Corn	455.9	35.9	Coffee	738.1	43.0
Wheat	227.0	17.9	Cut flowers and foliage	515.2	30.1
Soybeans	95.8	7.5	Bananas, including plantains, fresh or dried	200.7	11.7
Cotton	64.0	5.0	Coffee extracts	38.1	2.2
Soybean meal	63.1	5.0	Candies and chewing gum	26.5	1.5
Corn gluten meal	43.4	3.4	Crude animal material (glue stock)	25.8	1.5
Food preparations	37.4	2.9	Sugar, raw and refined	23.7	1.4
Soybean oil	26.4	2.1	Baked products and pastries	20.9	1.2
Pet food	21.9	1.7	Food preparations	15.4	0.9
Soybean flour	15.9	1.3	Tobacco products	15.0	0.9
Subtotal, top 10	1,050.6	82.7	Subtotal, top 10	1,619.5	94.5
All other agricultural products	219.9	17.3	All other agricultural products	95.1	5.5
Total	1,270.5	100.0	Total	1,714.6	100.0

Source: USDA, Economic Research Service using U.S. International Trade Commission's Dataweb.

U.S. agricultural imports from Colombia averaged $1.7 billion in 2007-09, making it the 12th largest agricultural exporter to the United States. Leading imports were coffee, cut flowers, bananas and plantains, coffee extracts, and candies and chewing gum. The United States ran a negative agricultural trade balance (more imports than exports) with Colombia, averaging over $440 million during 2007-09. The negative trade balance had been narrowing considerably in recent years but increased in 2009 as a result of the sharp drop in U.S. exports. Colombia had been a rapidly expanding market for U.S. agricultural exports until very recently, growing at a 40-percent annual rate between 2004 and 2008. In 2008-09, however, U.S. agricultural exports to Colombia dropped from $1.6 billion to $900 million, or 46 percent. In 2009, trade values declined worldwide as prices dropped from the high levels of 2008. Colombia was no exception, with its total agricultural imports in 2009 dropping 16 percent from the previous year. The U.S. share of Colombian imports also declined sharply, with much of this decline being filled by additional Colombian imports from the MERCOSUR countries, particularly Argentina and Brazil (fig. 3).

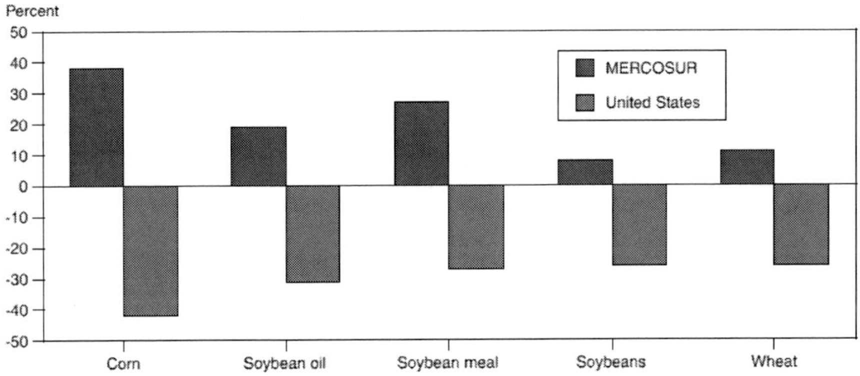

MERCOSUR = Common Market of the South.

Source: USDA, Economic Research Service using trade data in the Global Trade Atlas database.

Figure 3. Change in U.S. and MERCOSUR market shares in Colombia between 2008 and 2009.

Colombia has an FTA with the MERCOSUR countries, the agricultural provisions of which entered into force on January 1, 2009. In the case of corn, this allowed 2009 imports from Argentina and Brazil to pay a 7.6-percent duty while imports from the United States paid 15 percent (USDA, FAS, 2010b). In October 2010, the tariff on imports from the United States dropped to 5 percent, while that on imports from MERCOSUR countries dropped to zero, as the effect of higher international prices for corn produced a lower rate under the "price band" calculation (USDA, FAS, 2010c). [16] In the case of wheat imports, the tariff preference for MERCOSUR is even greater, with Argentine wheat entering duty free, while U.S. wheat pays a 17-percent duty (USDA, FAS, 2010a). The effect of the FTA between Colombia and the MERCOSUR countries on U.S. agricultural exports is clearly very different from that of the two ASEAN FTAs. In the case of ASEAN, a significant portion of U.S. exports already enters duty free, whereas all U.S. agricultural exports to Colombia face a duty. Further, a large portion of dutiable U.S. agricultural exports to ASEAN faced limited competition from China, Australia, or New Zealand. The most important U.S. exports to Colombia compete head-to-head with exports from MERCOSUR, and the tariffs MERCOSUR countries face have been declining gradually. In 2009, the margins of preference that

MERCOSUR imports receive finally started having an effect on the competitive position of the United States, a position that could soon be further eroded if the Canada-Colombia FTA and the EU-Colombia FTA enter into force and competing exports from these countries start receiving preferential treatment.

Agricultural Provisions of CTPA

Colombia currently applies tariff protection on all U.S. agricultural imports, with rates ranging from 5 to 80 percent. Under WTO rules, Colombia could raise these rates to their bound levels, which range from 15 to 227 percent. In addition, some agricultural products imported by Colombia are subject to additional duties imposed on top of the applied ad valorem tariff. This policy, which utilizes a price-band system to generate variable duties, is designed to keep domestic prices within a predetermined range. U.S. exports to Colombia that are subject to the price-band system include corn, wheat, rice, soybeans, pork, poultry, cheeses, and powdered milk.

Under the pending CTPA, the United States would receive immediate duty-free access on 78 percent of Colombian agricultural tariff lines accounting for almost 50 percent of 2007-09 U.S. agricultural exports to Colombia. This would apply to high-quality beef, wheat, soybeans, soybean meal, cotton, grapes, apples, pears, peaches, cherries, and many processed food products, including fruit juices, beer, wine, frozen french fries, breakfast cereals, and cookies. Colombia would eliminate most other tariffs on agricultural products within 15 years. Exceptions include poultry (spent fowl and chicken leg quarters) and rice, whose tariffs go to zero in 18 years and 19 years, respectively.

Other products whose tariff cuts would be subject to the longest implementation periods include pork, standard quality beef, corn, some fruits and vegetables, processed products, and dairy products. These also tend to be the products on which the highest applied rates are levied. The agreement would also provide duty-free TRQs on standard quality beef, variety meats, chicken leg quarters, spent fowl (chickens), dairy products, dried beans, corn, sorghum, glucose, pet food, animal feeds, rice, and soybean oil. The TA would also remove Colombia's price-band system upon implementation of the agreement. However, if the rates under the price-band system result in a rate below the MFN tariff, and this also happens to be lower than the preferential tariff under CTPA, the United States will be allowed to sell the product to Colombia at the lower rates.

The United States currently extends duty-free treatment to most imports from Colombia under the ATPA, a regional trade preference program. As a result, during 2007-09, 99.8 percent of Colombia's exports to the United States entered duty free. The pending CTPA would make these trade preferences permanent. During 2007-09, Colombia was assessed duties estimated at about $965,000 on U.S. imports of $9.8 million (USITC 2010 dataweb). The majority of dutiable trade occurred in sugar and sugar-containing products, dairy products, and tobacco. Currently, Colombian exports of these products are charged a duty if they exceed the U.S. TRQ quantities. Under the TA, the United States would provide additional duty-free TRQs on imports of Colombian beef, dairy products, tobacco, and sugar.[17] For the first three categories of products, the duty-free amounts increase over time, but within 15 years (less for some products), Colombia will have duty-free, quota-free access for all imports. In the case of sugar and specified sugar-containing products, the United States would triple Colombia's access to the U.S. sugar market in the first year of the agreement, from its historic 2.3-percent share of the U.S. raw cane sugar TRQ (25,273 metric tons), through the creation of an additional quota of 50,000 metric tons. Beginning in year 2, this new quota would expand by 750 metric tons annually in perpetuity. Sugar imports in excess of these quotas would continue to be charged the over-quota MFN tariff, which can exceed 100 percent in some years.

Potential Impact on U.S. Agricultural Exports

The United States has consistently had a trade deficit with Colombia over the past decade in both agricultural and nonagricultural goods. About 75 percent of imported agricultural products from Colombia consist of coffee beans and cut flowers that enter the United States with zero tariffs. Nearly 80 percent of nonagricultural imports from Colombia comprise coal and oil and face very low tariffs. The CTPA would narrow the trade deficit because of improved U.S. access to a more open market, while additional imports would be minimal because most products already enter the U.S. market duty free.

As previously discussed, the U.S. market share in Colombia has fallen for some commodities due to greater competition from Brazil and Argentina as well as from Canada and Chile. Despite increased competition and declining market share, total U.S. agricultural exports to Colombia are expected to be sustained at about $900 million per year through 2014 without the CTPA, as a result of continued strong global prices for grains and oilseeds, particularly corn.

It is likely that U.S. agricultural exports will benefit broadly with full implementation of the CTPA. This is because Colombia maintains sizeable tariffs across a wide spectrum of both bulk commodities and high-value products. Model results suggest that overall U.S. agricultural exports to Colombia will increase by 44 percent, or $370 million per year (table 12). The USITC estimates that U.S. agricultural exports to Colombia would grow by 24 percent, or $170 million per year (USITC, 2006). Jurenas (2009) cites a study by the American Farm Bureau Federation that estimates an annual increase of $693 million in U.S. agricultural exports to Colombia following implementation of the CTPA.

Table 12. Projected effect on U.S. exports to Colombia due to CTPA

	Tariff average	Base	Change	Percent change
		----$ millions----		
Rice	50.6	3.9	28.6	739.2
Wheat	12.5	149.0	90.1	60.5
Other grains	14.9	287.1	69.3	24.1
Fruits and vegetables	14.6	13.9	2.5	17.9
Oilseeds	10.1	67.6	18.1	26.7
Cotton	10	28.2	9.6	34.1
Beef	21.7	21.4	17.5	82.0
Poultry and pork	19.8	28.0	18.1	64.6
Other livestock products	13.7	6.2	2.4	38.1
Oilseed products	15.5	41.2	52.1	126.3
Dairy products	18.3	4.4	2.3	53.3
Processed foods	15	184.4	55.9	30.3
Other agricultural products	9.4	17.0	4.1	24.2
Total agriculture		852.2	370.7	43.5

CTPA = Colombia Trade Promotion Agreement.

Source: USDA, Economic Research Service results of Global Trade Analysis Project modeling exercise for this study; base year is 2014.

Among the Colombian grain sectors, rice is most heavily protected, with a tariff average of 51 percent. The United States would compete directly with rice exports from Peru and Ecuador in the Colombian market. U.S. rice exports to Colombia could increase annually by nearly $30 million, or about 740 percent, as a result of the elimination of the tariff on rice. In the last decade, the United States has been the leading supplier of wheat to Colombia.

Other suppliers include Canada and Argentina. The U.S. wheat share of the Colombian market has fallen since 2008, and this trend will likely continue as long as U.S. wheat faces a 17-percent tariff. However, with the CTPA, U.S. wheat exports to Colombia would likely increase by more than 60 percent, regaining some market share lost to Argentina and Canada.

The United States has traditionally been the major supplier of corn to Colombia. However, the United States is now facing significant competition from Argentina. In both 2009 and the first part of 2010, Colombia imported more corn from Argentina than it imported from the United States. This shift is due mainly from a price advantage Argentina enjoys as a result of tariff reductions for Argentine corn provided under the Colombia-Mercosur FTA. With the removal of the tariff, annual U.S. corn exports to Colombia would likely increase 24 percent, or about $70 million.

Despite having lost market share to Argentina and Paraguay in the Colombian soybean market in 2010, the United States continues to be the leading supplier of soybeans to Colombia. The United States also has remained the leading supplier of cotton to Colombia. Given that the United States is the dominant supplier and tariffs are relatively low, the removal of tariffs would modestly expand U.S. exports of both soybeans and cotton.

Colombia has maintained high tariffs on most livestock products, including beef, poultry, pork, and dairy products. The United States supplies about 50 percent of Colombia's beef (including fats of bovine origin), with the remainder coming from other South American countries. It is likely that U.S. exports of beef to Colombia will rise by more than 80 percent after the elimination of tariffs in the CTPA. The United States competes directly with Chile and Canada for exports of pork to Colombia. Currently, U.S. pork and poultry meat faces an average MFN tariff of nearly 20 percent in Colombia. The elimination of tariffs on U.S. exports would likely increase U.S. exports of these products by more than 60 percent. The MFN tariff faced by U.S. dairy product exports to Colombia currently averages about 18 percent. The scheduled elimination of these tariffs is estimated to increase U.S. exports by an additional 50 percent.

Colombian demand for soybean meal has grown as a result of increased feed demand by the country's poultry sector. However, the U.S. share of Colombia's soybean meal market plummeted from 60 percent in 2008 to 8 percent in 2010, whereas Argentina increased its share from 31 to 84 percent over the same period. The United States faces an average tariff for oilseed products of nearly 16 percent in the Colombian market. The full implementation of the CTPA would likely more than double U.S. exports of oilseed products and make them more competitive with Argentina's exports.

Colombia's imports of processed food products comprise a wide array of items, including confectionery products and ingredients used in Colombia's food manufacturing industry. The United States faces an average tariff of 15 percent on processed food items. Elimination of the tariff from the CTPA would likely increase U.S. exports of these products to Colombia by 30 percent, or $52 million per year.

U.S. agricultural imports from Colombia would increase about 6 percent, or $117 million per year, following implementation of the CTPA (table 13). Nearly all of the increase would be from an expansion of the U.S. sugar quota, accounting for $108 million over a 10-year period. U.S. dairy imports would also increase following the elimination of over-quota tariffs on Colombian dairy products. This would likely result in an annual increase of about $3 million in additional U.S. dairy imports from Colombia.

Table 13. Projected effect on U.S. imports from Colombia due to CTPA

	Tariff average	Base	Change	Percent change
		----$ millions----		
Rice	0.0	0.2	0.01	6.5
Wheat	0.0	0.0	0.00	0.0
Other grains	0.0	0.2	0.00	2.5
Fruits and vegetables	0.0	233.2	0.03	0.0
Oilseeds	0.0	0.0	0.02	0.0
Cotton	0.0	0.1	0.02	38.0
Beef	0.0	0.3	0.04	14.1
Poultry and pork	0.0	0.7	0.01	2.0
Other livestock products	0.0	23.9	0.29	1.2
Oilseed products	0.0	4.3	0.57	13.3
Dairy products	41.2	1.5	2.78	181.8
Processed foods	0.0	320.2	5.02	1.6
Other agricultural products	0.0	1,467.3	107.72	7.3
Total agriculture		2,048.0	116.53	5.7

CTPA = Colombia Trade Promotion Agreement.

Source: USDA, Economic Research Service results of Global Trade Analysis Project modeling exercise for this study; base year is 2014.

The U.S.-Panama Trade Promotion Agreement (PTPA)

Structure of agricultural trade

The United States runs a positive agricultural trade balance with Panama, averaging over $330 million per year during 2007-09, which helps rank Panama as 45th among overseas U.S. markets (table 14). Leading U.S. exports to Panama were corn, soybean meal, wheat, rice, and food preparations, which together accounted for over 55 percent of all U.S. sales. The United States accounted for almost 50 percent of Panama's $2.5 billion agricultural imports during this period. Major U.S. competitors for trade with Panama were Costa Rica, Mexico, and Guatemala.

U.S. imports from Panama averaged $52 million per year during 2007-09, placing Panama 65th as a supplier of agricultural commodities to the United States. Leading U.S. imports were sugar, coffee, pineapple, melons, and bananas.

Agricultural Provisions of PTPA

During 2007-09, one-third of U.S. agricultural exports entered Panama's market duty free, including soybeans, soymeal, wheat, and fresh grapes. About one-half of the remaining exports faced tariffs between 1 and 15 percent, but some key products were subject to much higher rates, including corn at 40 percent, rice at 90 percent, and chicken leg quarters at 260 percent. Under PTPA, an additional 24 percent of U.S. agricultural exports to Panama would receive immediate duty-free treatment, including high-quality beef, mechanically deboned chicken, frozen whole turkeys and turkey breasts, pork variety meats, whey, crude vegetable oils, most fresh fruits (including apples and pears), almonds, walnuts, raisins, prunes, many processed food products (including soups and chocolate confectionery), distilled spirits, wine, and pet food. Currently, the tariffs on these items entering Panama range from 5 to 15 percent.

Under PTPA, Panama agreed to establish preferential TRQs for imports of U.S. pork, lard, specified processed pork products, chicken leg quarters, specified dairy products, fresh potatoes, frozen french fries, onions, corn, rice, refined corn oil, dried beans, and tomato paste. Quotas for these import-sensitive commodities would be phased out in 5 to 20 years. The longest transition period (20 years) would apply to rice, Panama's most sensitive agricultural commodity. However, Panama agreed to increase duty-free access for U.S. rice if needed to cover a shortfall in domestic output. Border protection on U.S. chicken leg quarters would end in year 18. Quotas to be created for fresh or chilled onion and fresh or chilled potatoes would expand by 2 percent annually in perpetuity with MFN over-quota tariffs applying to imports that exceed quota amounts.

Table 14. Composition of U.S. agricultural trade with Panama, 2007-09 averages

Product	Main U.S. exports		Product	Main U.S. imports	
	Value	Share of total		Value	Share of total
	$ millions	*Percent*		*$ millions*	*Percent*
Corn	75.5	19.7	Sugar, raw and refined	17.1	33.0
Soybean meal	50.7	13.2	Coffee	12.3	23.7
Wheat	33.9	8.8	Fresh or dried pineapples	5.7	10.9
Food preparations	33.0	8.6	Fresh melons (excluding watermelons)	3.3	6.4
Rice	20.6	5.4	Nonalcoholic beverages	2.2	4.3
Grain products	14.0	3.7	Fresh or chilled pumpkins and squash	2.1	4.1
Cocoa beans and products	14.0	3.6	Bananas, including plantains, fresh or dried	2.0	3.8
Vegetables: preparations	7.3	1.9	Baked products and pastries	1.9	3.7
Whiskies	7.3	1.9	Rum and taffia	0.9	1.7
Cheese	6.9	1.8	Cocoa beans and products	0.9	1.6
Subtotal, top 10	263.2	68.6	Subtotal, top 10	48.4	93.2
All other agricultural products	120.5	31.4	All other agricultural products	3.5	6.8
Total	383.8	100.0	Total	52.0	100.0

Source: USDA, Economic Research Service using U.S. International Trade Commission's Dataweb.

Almost all of Panama's agricultural exports to the United States already enter duty free under the CBERA trade preference program. Under PTPA, the United States would provide additional duty-free TRQs on imports of Panamanian dairy products and sugar. For dairy products, the duty-free amounts increase over time, and after 15-17 years, Panama will have duty-free, quota-free access for all dairy imports. In the case of sugar and specified sugar-containing products, the United States would increase Panama's access to the U.S. sugar market in the first year of the agreement, from its historic 2.7-percent share of the U.S. raw cane sugar TRQ (30,540 metric tons), through the creation of two additional quotas of 505 (on raw and refined sugar and syrups) and 6,060 metric tons (on raw cane sugar). Beginning in year two, these new quotas would expand annually by 5 and 60 metric tons, respectively, for 10 years. The larger of the two quotas would then be capped at 6,600 metric tons, while the smaller would continue to increase by 5 metric tons per year in perpetuity. Sugar imports in excess of these quotas would continue to be charged the over-quota MFN tariff, which can exceed 100 percent in some years.

Potential Impact on U.S. Agricultural Exports

Panama's trade flow data in the GTAP model are biased by the large quantities of imports and exports passing through the country's Colon Free Zone. This made it impracticable to use GTAP for this analysis.

The USITC employed a partial equilibrium model that simulates the effects of changes to tariffs and TRQs on trade between the United States and Panama in specified goods (USITC, 2007b). It estimated that annual U.S. exports of agricultural commodities and processed foods to Panama would be $46 million higher (or about 20 percent above the 2006 level) when the agreement is fully implemented. This increase was largely attributed to gains in exports of rice ($13.8 million), corn ($7 million), processed foods ($9.6 million), frozen potatoes ($1 million), and meats ($4.4 million). Given the size of the tariffs currently levied on these products and the share of the Panamanian import market currently accounted for by U.S. exports, we believe these figures are within the ranges we would expect as a result of implementing the PTPA.

Conclusion

The principal objective of bilateral and regional free trade agreements is to secure trade liberalization and expand market access for members. But the discriminatory nature of FTAs may result in FTA members expanding their trade at the expense of nonmembers, who may become less competitive purely on the basis of facing a higher tariff than the members.

Most studies of the effects of FTAs find that trade diversion is less apparent than might be expected. While overall trade diversion does not appear to be a major concern in the economic literature, within some agreements or within specific sectors of some agreements, it can be significant. This study finds that in the case of the recently implemented FTAs between the ASEAN countries and China, Australia, and New Zealand, the potential for U.S. agricultural exporters to be affected as a result of trade diversion is modest. This is because a large portion of U.S. exports to these countries already faces duty-free or minimal tariffs. Where tariffs are significant, the United States often faces only minimal competition from FTA members.

By contrast, our analysis of the pending U.S. trade agreement with Colombia reveals a different story. Colombia has been active in negotiating additional FTAs with some key U.S. competitors. One of these FTAs, with the four members of MERCOSUR, has already had significant effects on U.S. agricultural exports and market shares in the Colombian market. A majority of U.S. agricultural exports to Colombia compete head-to-head with exports from MERCOSUR countries. The U.S. market position in Colombia could soon be further eroded if the Canada-Colombia FTA and the EU-Colombia FTA enter into force and competing exports from these countries receive duty-free treatment. Duty-free access to the Colombian market would help maintain and improve the competitive position of U.S. producers.

Korea is also negotiating FTAs with the EU and Australia, two important competitors of the United States in the Korean market. In beef exports, where large U.S. gains are expected from a U.S-Korea trade agreement, the United States competes with Australia. Likewise, in pork and processed foods, two additional expected sources of U.S. export gains, the United States competes directly with the EU.

Exports are very important to U.S. agriculture. While the overall scale of gains in an individual trade agreement is limited compared with the potential gains in a multilateral agreement, U.S. trade agreements can, indeed, provide opportunities for additional U.S. agricultural sales overseas. Model results indicate that U.S. agricultural exports would increase by $1.9 billion per year if KORUS was implemented, $370 million per year if the CTPA was implemented, and $46 million if the PTPA was implemented.

REFERENCES

Blustein, Paul (2009). *Misadventures of the Most Favored Nations*. Public Affairs Books: New York.

Burfisher, Mary E., and Steven Zahniser (2003). "Multilateralism and Regionalism – Dual Strategies for Trade Reform," *Amber Waves*, Vol. 1, Issue 4. U.S. Department of Agriculture, Economic Research Service, www.ers.usda.gov/amberwaves/september03/features/multilateralism.htm

Cooper, William H., Mark E. Manyin, Remy Jurenas, and Michaela D. Platzer (2009). *The Proposed South Korea-U.S. Free Trade Agreement (KORUS FTA): Provisions and Implications*. Congressional Research Service RL34330.

Fabiosa, Jacinto F., Dermot J. Hayes, and Fengxia Dong (2007). "Impact of the South Korea-U.S. Free Trade Agreement on the U.S. Livestock Sector." Working Paper 07-WP 455. Center of Agricultural and Rural Development, Iowa State University.

Francois, Joseph, Miriam Manchin, Hanna Norberg, and Annette Pelkmans (2009). *Trade Impact Assessment (Trade SIA) of an EU-ASEAN Free Trade Agreement*. Research Report 200908-01. Institute for International & Development Economics.

Francois, Joseph F., Bradley J. McDonald, and Hakan Nordstrom (1996). *Liberalization and Capital Accumulation in the GTAP Model*. GTAP Technical Paper No. 7. Center for Global Trade Analysis, Purdue University.

Freund, Caroline, and Emanuel Ornelas (2010). "Regional Trade Agreements." World Bank Policy Research Working Paper 5314.

Gehlhar, M. (1997). "Historical Analysis of Growth and Trade Patterns in the Pacific Rim": An Evaluation of the GTAP Framework," in T.W. Hertel (ed.), *Global Trade Analysis: Modeling and Applications*. Cambridge University Press: Cambridge, MA.

Global Trade Information Services (2010). Global Trade Atlas and World Trade Atlas databases.

Harrison, W.J., and K.R. Pearson (1996). "Computing Solutions for Large General Equilibrium Models Using GEMPACK." *Computational Economics*, Vol. 9, pp. 83-127.

Hertel, T., and M. Tsigas (1997). "The Structure of GTAP," in Hertel, T. (ed.), *Global Trade Analysis*. Cambridge University Press: Cambridge, MA.

Hornbeck, J.F. (2005). *The Proposed U.S.-Panama Free Trade Agreement*. Congressional Research Service RL32540.

Jurenas, Remy (2009). *Agriculture in Pending U.S. Free Trade Agreements with Colombia, Panama, and South Korea*. Congressional Research Service R40622.

Korea Customs Service (2010). Korea Customs Tariff Database, http://english.customs.go.kr/kcsweb/user.tdf?a=user.customtariff.CustomTariffApp&c=1001&mc=ENGLISH_INFORMATION_KOREA

Krugman, Paul (1991). "Is Bilateralism Bad?" in E. Helpman and A. Razin (eds.), *International Trade and Trade Policy*. MIT Press: Cambridge, MA.

Mai, Yinhua, Philip Adams, Mingtai Fan, Ronglin Li, and Zhaoyang Zheng (2005). *Modeling the Potential Benefits of an Australia-China Free Trade Agreement*. The Centre of Policy Studies, Monash University, Melbourne, Australia.

Narayanan, B.G., and T.L. Walmsley (2008). *Global Trade, Assistance, and Production: The GTAP 7 Data Base*. Center for Global Trade Analysis, Purdue University.

U.S. International Trade Commission (USITC) (2006). *U.S.-Colombia Trade Promotion Agreement: Potential Economy-wide and Selected Sectoral Effects*. USITC Publication 3896.

U.S. International Trade Commission (USITC) (2007a). *U.S.-Korea Free Trade Agreement: Potential Economy-wide and Selected Sectoral Effects*. USITC Publication 3949.

U.S. International Trade Commission (USITC) (2007b). *U.S.-Panama Trade Promotion Agreement: Potential Economy-wide and Selected Sectoral Effects*. USITC Publication 3948.

U.S. International Trade Commission (USITC) (2010). U.S. Imports/Exports Data. http://dataweb.usitc.gov/

U.S. Department of Agriculture, Foreign Agricultural Service (2010a). *Colombia's Looming FTA With Canada Is Bad News for U.S. Wheat Exports*. GAIN Rep. No. 8-6-2010.

U.S. Department of Agriculture, Foreign Agricultural Service (2010b). *Colombia Grain and Feed Annual*. GAIN Rep. No. 3-10-2010.

U.S. Department of Agriculture, Foreign Agricultural Service (2010c). *U.S. Corn Tariff Dropped to Five Percent*. GAIN Rep. No. 10-29-2010.

Villarreal, M. Angeles (2010). *The Proposed U.S.-Colombia Free Trade Agreement: Economic and Political Implications*. Congressional Research Service RL34470.

World Trade Organization (WTO) (2009). *Overview of Developments in the International Trading Environment*. WT/TPR/OV/12.

APPENDIX 1. PROJECTING A 2014 BENCHMARK

The FTAs in this report are agreements in which preferential trade liberalization is undertaken reciprocally between the participating countries. The GTAP modeling framework provides a useful tool for assessing effects of FTAs because it is comprised of explicit bilateral trade flows between the United States and all trading partners. The model captures domestic and foreign economic activity for all countries and in all goods and services. Impacts of an FTA depend most importantly on pre-existing trade flows and the reduction in tariffs and TRQs.

Because the data are historical in the GTAP framework, this can misrepresent current trade patterns. The current public release of the GTAP Data Base (version 7) depicts the world economy as of 2004. Since 2004, there have been several global economic shocks affecting trade, including increased energy and agricultural commodity prices, a worldwide financial crisis, and outbreaks of livestock diseases. Global trade patterns have also shifted considerably with China's ongoing rapid economic growth. Also supporting U.S. agricultural exports is the cumulative effect of the depreciated U.S. dollar. This depreciation of the dollar makes U.S. agricultural exports increasingly competitive in international markets. U.S. agricultural exports rose from $62 billion in 2004 to $108 billion in 2010. There are also commodity-specific shifts in trade patterns. Trade in meat has changed dramatically since 2004. This is especially true for exports of beef and other meat exports to Korea. Despite beef exports hampered by BSE (Bovine Spongiform Encephalopathy) restrictions, U.S. agricultural exports to Korea have nearly doubled since 2004.

One of the challenges of assessing pending TAs is that it is not possible to predict exactly when each TA will be ratified. In addition, there is also a "phase-in" period once a TA is signed into law. Assumptions regarding the approximate timing are needed to quantify the effects of TAs. It is assumed that if ratified TAs were to be implemented in the near future, most tariffs would be reduced by 2014. In this study, the year 2014 serves as a benchmark year for the analysis of the pending U.S. TAs with Korea and Colombia.

The GTAP framework can be used to generate a future base period by simulating economic growth over several years, and it can be used to simulate the effect of policy reforms in a future year. In this study, we perform a growth simulation to update the base year period prior to performing trade policy simulations for TAs. This is done by using predetermined rates of economic growth for all regions. In doing so, we use the model to establish a new benchmark year (2014) and for estimating the future effects of the TAs being phased in beyond 2014. To assess the impact of pending TAs, it was necessary in this study to simulate world trade, production, and consumption as they would likely appear in 2014, when implementation of TAs might take place provided the agreements are ratified. The re-benchmarking of GTAP was taken in two steps. First, macroeconomic variables are updated for all countries and sub-regions in the model. This information was drawn from USDA's macroeconomic projections (USDA, 2010). Gross domestic product and population changes are based on observed changes from 2004 to 2009 with projections made from 2010 to 2014 (tables A1.1 and A1.2). Macroeconomic assumptions underlying USDA's long-term projections reflect a slow transition back toward steady growth at longrun sustainable rates in 2011 and beyond. Global growth is projected to average 3.3 percent in 2010 through 2014. The accelerated growth is mostly due to high growth rates in emerging market countries such as China and India. Each country/region reaches a predetermined GDP level in 2014. In the growth simulation GDP, the economy-wide stock of capital and labor supply are exogenous while total factor productivity is endogenous. In general, developing countries are the main source of growth in world agricultural demand and trade. Income growth in developing countries increases the demand for food more than in developed countries because a larger share of income is devoted to food consumption.

Table A1.1. Gross domestic product levels and growth rates

	2004	2009	2014	Annual growth, 2004-09	Annual growth, 2009-14
		$ billions		*Percent change*	
United States	12,264	13,006	14,917	1.2	2.8
Korea	813	927	1,123	2.7	3.9
Colombia	114	140	166	4.2	3.5
Panama	15	21	29	7.6	6.8
EU 27	13,376	13,896	15,064	0.8	1.6
China	2,084	3,339	4,999	9.9	8.4
India	699	1,018	1,469	7.8	7.6
Other Latin America	2,520	2,930	3,537	3.1	3.8
Other Asia and Oceania	7,432	7,921	9,075	1.3	2.8
Rest of world	4,200	4,936	5,970	3.3	3.9
World	43,515	48,134	56,349	2.0	3.2

Source: USDA, Economic Research Service.

Table A1.2. Population level and growth rates

	2004	2009	2014	Annual growth, 2004-09	Annual growth, 2009-14
		Millions		*Percent change*	
United States	293	307	322	0.96	0.97
Korea	48	49	49	0.27	0.22
Colombia	41	44	46	1.31	1.15
Panama	3	3	4	1.60	1.43
EU 27	488	492	494	0.14	0.08
China	1,299	1,339	1,385	0.60	0.68
India	1,074	1,157	1,236	1.50	1.34
Other Latin America	505	539	571	1.30	1.18
Other Asia and Oceania	1,151	1,222	1,291	1.21	1.09
Rest of world	1,485	1,617	1,754	1.71	1.65
World	6,387	6,768	7,153	1.16	1.11

Source: USDA, Economic Research Service.

The second step of the benchmarking exercise is to realign commodity-specific trade flows to better reflect observed trends in trade flows. Although income growth provides the foundation for world demand and trade for agricultural products, in some cases commodity shifts in trade take place for other reasons. For example, a gradual recovery took place for U.S. beef exports to Japan and Korea, which were markets that were closed to the United States following the first U.S. case of bovine spongiform encephalopathy (BSE). U.S. exports of beef to Korea were set at their 2003 level for 2014 (app. fig. 1). Korea also became Asia's fastest growth market for pork with its imports accounting for one-fifth of the increase in world pork imports. Increasing per capita consumption of poultry in Korea, combined with environmental restrictions on expanding production in Korea is contributing to strong import growth. Global trade in soybean and soybean products has risen rapidly since 2004, surpassing both the volume of wheat and coarse grains. U.S. exports of soybeans rose from 25 million tons in 2004 to 40 million tons in 2009, largely from strong demand in China. Argentina is now the dominant supplier of soybean meal and soybean oil exports and continues to increase its share in the world market. Alterations to reflect these fundamental changes were made to the GTAP trade data to better depict trade patterns for the year 2014.

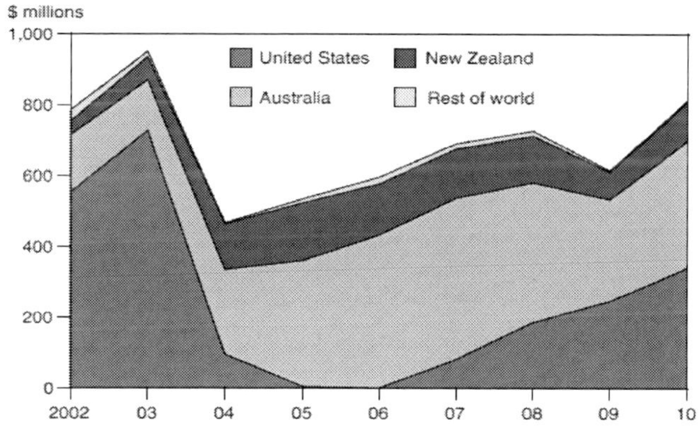

Source: USDA, Economic Research Service using trade data in the Global Trade Atlas database.

Appendix figure 1. Korean beef imports.

APPENDIX 2. TABLES

Table A2.1. ASEAN FTAs, summary of tariff line commitments[1]

	Bound duty free		Duty free in first year[2]		Duty free by last year[3]		Partially liberalized[2]		Excluded		Total tariff lines	
	No.	Pct.	No.	Pct.	No.	Pct.	No.	Pct.	No.	Pct.	No.	Pct.
ASEAN-China												
China	70	6	963	87	0	0	50	5	22	2	1,105	100
Indonesia	0	0	1,091	93	0	0	0	0	85	7	1,176	100
Malaysia	107	9	1,050	87	0	0	13	1	33	3	1,203	100
Philippines	0	0	1,045	82	70	5	32	3	130	10	1,277	100
Thailand	29	2	1,057	87	0	0	66	5	67	5	1,219	100
Vietnam	95	9	341	31	663	60	0	0	0	0	1,099	100
ASEAN-Australia/New Zealand												
Australia	231	31	524	69	2	0	0	0	0	0	757	100
New Zealand	460	45	544	53	19	2	0	0	0	0	1,023	100
Indonesia	0	0	990	79	113	9	63	5	92	7	1,258	100
Malaysia	107	9	886	74	127	11	20	2	65	5	1,205	100
Philippines	0	0	549	43	624	49	72	6	36	3	1,281	100
Thailand	29	2	460	38	623	51	0	0	107	9	1,219	100
Vietnam	95	8	33	3	954	81	76	6	24	2	1,182	100

ASEAN = Association of Southeast Asian Nations. FTA = free trade agreement.

[1] The table contains a count of simple tariff lines (not trade weighted) at the tariff line level (the HS8-digit level for China, the Philippines, Thailand, Australia, and New Zealand; the HS9 digit level for Malaysia; and the HS10-digit level for Indonesia and Vietnam).

[2] Includes cuts made under the Early Harvest Program.

[3] Duties that are cut to zero by the end of the FTA's implementation period.

Source: USDA, Economic Research Service.

Table A2.2. Sensitive tariff lines under the ASEAN-Australia/New Zealand and ASEAN-China FTAs

ASEAN country tariff lines excluded from cuts or partially liberalized under the ASEAN-Australia/New Zealand FTA

IBAT description	Indonesia				Malaysia				Philippines				Thailand				Vietnam			
	Avg. tariff	No. of lines	TRQ lines	No. cut	Avg. tariff	No. of lines	TRQ lines	No. cut	Avg. tariff	No. of lines	TRQ lines	No. cut	Avg. tariff	No. of lines	TRQ lines	No. cut	Avg. tariff	No. of lines	TRQ lines	No. cut
Ag products: misc	85.0	2																		
Beverages: beer	40.0	2		2	410.5	2		2									40.0	2		
Beverages: brandy	170.0	4		4	470.7	2		2									40.0	4		
Beverages: cider	143.3	6		6	421.9	8		8									40.0	5		
Beverages: distilled spirits nes	137.1	17		17	611.0	11		11									29.7	17		
Beverages: gin	170.0	2		2	1,014.5	1		1									40.0	2		
Beverages: nonalcoholic													20.0	4	4	4				
Beverages: rum	170.0	2		2	1,109.8	1		1									40.0	2		
Beverages: whiskey	170.0	2		2	372.0	1		1									40.0	2		
Beverages: wine	148.7	15		15	180.1	8		8									28.0	15		
Cocoa powde									5.0	1										
Coffee husks & skins													30.0	2	2	2				
Coffee mixtures & extracts													40.0	3	3	3				
Coffee: not roasted													30.0	4	4	4				
Coffee: roasted													30.0	4	4	4				
Crude animal material	7.5	1																		
Crude vegetable material													30.0	1	1	1	5.0	2		2
Dairy: butter									5.0	1										
Dairy: cheese	4.0	2																		
Dairy: fluid milk & cream	4.0	2											20.0	3	3	3				
Dairy: milk & cream, pwdr & cndnsd	4.0	4	4										20.0	2	2	2				
Dairy: other milk products	4.0	3							5.0	1										
Eggs					5.0	4	4	4												
Feed: pet food									5.0	3										
Feed: waste & residues nes																	5.0	1		
Fiber: silk													30.0	1	1	1				
Food prep: composite mixtures	85.0	8																		
Fruit (dried & frsh): coconuts													20.0	2	2	2				
Fruit (frsh): avocados & mangoes	8.3	2			5.0	3														
Fruit (frsh): bananas	4.0	1			5.0	5														
Fruit (frsh): berries	4.0	1																		
Fruit (frsh): citrus nes	18.8	1															32.0	1		
Fruit (frsh): melons					5.0	4														
Fruit (frsh): pineapples	4.0	1			9.0	1														
Grain prod: breakfast cereal									5.0	1										
Grain prod: flour (non-wheat)	9.0	1		1																
Grain prod: meal									5.0	1										
Grain prod: starch (corn)									5.0	1										
Grain: corn	5.0	1		1					34.0	2	2		20.0	2	2	2				
Grain: rice (unmilled)	21.8	4	4	4	40.0	4		4	50.0	6	6	6	30.0	3	3	3				
Hort: flowers & foilage (cut)	7.5	3											5.0	5						
Hort: plants (live)	5.0	4																		
Live animals (other)	5.0	1		1																

ASEAN country tariff lines excluded from cuts or partially liberalized under the ASEAN-Australia/New Zealand FTA

	Indonesia				Malaysia				Philippines				Thailand				Vietnam			
IBAT description	Avg. tariff	No. of lines	TRQ lines	No. cut	Avg. tariff	No. of lines	TRQ lines	No. cut	Avg. tariff	No. of lines	TRQ lines	No. cut	Avg. tariff	No. of lines	TRQ lines	No. cut	Avg. tariff	No. of lines	TRQ lines	No. cut
Live bovine	2.5	1																		
Live sheep & goats									5.0	2	2									
Meat (frsh or frzn): edible offal	2.5	1							4.0	1										
Meat (frsh or frzn): goat	2.5	1							5.0	2	2									
Meat (frsh or frzn): sheep	3.8	4		2																
Meat (frsh): pork									28.0	6	6									
Meat (frsh): poultry									5.0	2	2						12.5	6		3
Meat (frzn): beef	5.0	1		1																
Meat (frzn): pork	3.8	1							28.0	10	10									
Meat (frzn): poultry	12.5	1							23.7	13	13						17.9	7		6
Meat (prep): beef																	5.0	1		
Meat (prep): nes									18.5	2							5.0	3		
Meat (prep): pork									28.1	7							5.0	8		
Meat (prep): poultry									32.0	3							5.0	4		
Nuts & fruit (dried & frsh) nes	4.0	1			5.0	7							30.0	1	1	1				
Oil seeds: copra													20.0	1	1	1				
Oil seeds: other																	10.0	1		1
Oil seeds: soybeans	10.0	1		1									20.0	2	2	2				
Oil: coconut													20.0	4	4	4				
Oil: palm													20.0	3	3	3				
Oil: palm kernal													20.0	7	7	7				
Oil: soybean													20.0	4	4	4				
Oilcake: soybeans													20.0	1	1	1				
Spices													27.0	6	6	6				
Starches (edible nes)									5.0	1										
Sweeteners: beet & cane sugar (raw)	24.8	3		3					53.8	4	4	4	65.0	2	2	2				
Sweeteners: beet & cane sugar (refined)	36.8	4		4					32.2	14	14	14	65.0	4	4	4				
Sweeteners: honey	4.0	1																		
Tea													30.0	8	8	8				
Tobacco (unmanufactured)					5.0	5	5	5					60.0	12	12	12				
Tobacco products	10.6	16		9	120.6	14		14									35.9	17		12
Veg (dried): onion, garlic, leeks													27.0	1	1	1				
Veg (dried): other													27.0	1	1	1				
Veg (frsh): cabbage	4.0	5							20.0	2										
Veg (frsh): carrots & edible roots		2							32.0	1										
Veg (frsh): garlic & leeks									5.02				27.0	2	2	2				
Veg (frsh): lettuce	4.0	1							20.0	2										
Veg (frsh): onions & shallots	12.5	1							5.0	2			43.5	4	4	4				
Veg (frsh): other	4.0	1							16.0	1										
Veg (frsh): potatoes	18.8	1							32.0	2	2		27.0	2	2	2				
Veg (frsh): tomatoes	4.0	1																		
Totals		155	23	92		05	9	65		108	75	36		107	102	102		100	0	24
		555	209	319																

Table A2.2. (Continued)

China and ASEAN tariff lines excluded from cuts or partially liberalized under the ASEAN-China FTA

IBAT description	Indonesia				Malaysia				Philippines				Thailand				Vietnam			
	Avg. tariff	No. of lines	TRQ lines	No. cut	Avg. tariff	No. of lines	TRQ lines	No. cut	Avg. tariff	No. of lines	TRQ lines	No. cut	Avg. tariff	No. of lines	TRQ lines	No. cut	Avg. tariff	No. of lines	TRQ lines	No. cut
Ag products: misc	150.0	2		2																
Beverages: beer	40.0	2		2																
Beverages: brandy	150.0	4		4																
Beverages: cider	138.0	5		5																
Beverages: distilled spirits nes	121.8	17		17																
Beverages: gin	150.0	2		2																
Beverages: nonalcoholic													50.0	8	8					
Beverages: rum	150.0	2		2																
Beverages: whiskey	150.0	2		2																
Beverages: wine	134.0	15		15																
Coffee husks & skins													44.0	2	2	2				
Coffee mixtures & extracts													40.0	3	3	3				
Coffee: not roasted													30.0	4	4	4	5.0	2		
Coffee: roasted													30.0	4	4	4	5.0	1		
Crude vegetable material													1.0	2	2	2				
Dairy: fluid milk & cream					35.0	12	12	12					40.0	3	3	3				
Dairy: milk & cream, pwdr & cndnsd													5.0	2	2	2				
Eggs					50.0	4	4	4					5.0	2						
Feed: pet food									29.7	6		6	5.0	9						
Fiber: animal hair, excl wool																	5.0	1	1	
Fiber: cotton (carded)																	40.0	1	1	1
Fiber: cotton (not carded)																	5.0	1	1	
Fiber: silk													226.0	1	1	1				
Fiber: wool																	5.0	5	5	
Food prep: composite mixtures	150.0	5		5													5.0	1		
Fruit (dried & frsh): coconuts													50.0	2	2					
Fruit (prep): composite mixtures									5.0	1										
Fruit (prep): pineapples																	5.0	2		
Fruit juice: mixtures													5.0	3						
Fruit juice: pineapple																	5.0	2		
Grain prod: breakfast cereal																	50.0	1	1	
Grain prod: flour (non-wheat)	9.0	1		1													16.7	3	3	1
Grain prod: flour (wheat)													5.0	2			50.0	1	1	
Grain prod: meal																	32.0	5	5	
Grain prod: starch (corn)									5.0	1										
Grain: corn	5.0	2		2					42.5	2	2	2	20.0	2	2	2	35.0	2	2	1
Grain: rice (milled)	160.0	6	6	6	40.0	4		4	45.0	12	12	12	50.0	6	6		27.5	4	4	
Grain: rice (unmilled)	160.0	3	3	3	40.0	4		4	45.0	6	6	6	50.0	3	3		50.0	6	6	
Grain: wheat																	5.0	3	3	
Live pigs									32.5	4	4	4								
Live poultry					30.0	2	2	2	36.3	4	4	4								
Meat (frsh): pork									35.0	10	10	10								
Meat (frsh): poultry					40.0	2	2	2	39.0	10	10	10								

China and ASEAN tariff lines excluded from cuts or partially liberalized under the ASEAN-China FTA

IBAT description	Indonesia				Malaysia				Philippines				Thailand				Vietnam			
	Avg. tariff	No. of lines	TRQ lines	No. cut	Avg. tariff	No. of lines	TRQ lines	No. cut	Avg. tariff	No. of lines	TRQ lines	No. cut	Avg. tariff	No. of lines	TRQ lines	No. cut	Avg. tariff	No. of lines	TRQ lines	No. cut
Meat (frzn): pork									35.0	10	10	10								
Meat (frzn): poultry					40.0	2	2	2	31.3	24	24	20								
Meat (prep): pork									40.0	6		6	5.0	4						
Meat (prep): poultry									40.0	3	0	3								
Nuts & fruit (dried & frsh) nes													50.0	1	1					
Nuts & fruit (prepared) nes													5.0	5			5.0	1		
Oil seeds: copra													36.0	1	1	1				
Oil seeds: soybeans													80.0	2	2	2				
Oil: coconut													20.0	4	4	4				
Oil: palm													20.0	3	3	3	8.8	4	4	4
Oil: palm kernal													20.0	7	7	7				
Oil: rape																	9.0	5	5	5
Oil: soybean													50.0	4	4		9.0	2	2	2
Oilcake: soybeans													5.0	1	1	1				
Spices									5.0	4			27.0	6	6	6	5.0	2		
Starches (edible nes)									5.0	1										
Sweeteners: beet & cane sugar (raw)									50.0	4	4	3	50.0	2	2		50.0	2	2	2
Sweeteners: beet & cane sugar (refined)									29.0	14	14	11	50.0	4	4		50.0	4	4	4
Tea													30.0	8	8	8				
Tobacco (unmanufactured)	5.0	10		10	5.0	1	1	1					30.0	12	12	12	5.0	5		
Tobacco products					46.8	14		1									34.2	6		2
Veg (dried & frsh): roots & tubers									40.0	4		4								
Veg (dried): onion, garlic, leeks													50.0	1	1					
Veg (frsh): beans & peas									5.0	2										
Veg (frsh): cabbage					90.0	1	1	1	30.0	3		3								
Veg (frsh): carrots & edible roots									21.7	3		2								
Veg (frsh): cucumbers									5.0	1										
Veg (frsh): garlic & leeks									22.5	4		2	50.0	2	2					
Veg (frsh): lettuce									5.0	4										
Veg (frsh): onions & shallots									40.0	4		4	50.0	4	4					
Veg (frsh): other									5.0	5										
Veg (frsh): potatoes									40.0	2	2	2	50.0	2	2					
Veg (frzn or prep): other									18.8	8		6								
Veg (prep): tomatoes													5.0	2						
Totals		78	9	78		46	24	33		162	102	130		133	106	67		72	50	22
		491	291	330																

ASEAN = Association of Southeast Asian Nations. FTA = free trade agreement. nes = not elsewhere specified. TRQ = tariff-rate quota.

Source: USDA, Economic Research Service calculations using USDA internal databases.

Table A2.3. Three U.S. pending trade agreements, summary of tariff line commitments[1]

	Bound duty free		Duty free in first year		Duty free by last year		Partially liberalized[2]		Excluded		Total tariff lines	
	No.	*Pct.*	*No.*	*Pct.*	*No.*	*Pct.*	*No.*	*Pct.*	*No.*	*Pct.*	*No.*	*Pct.*
U.S.-Korea												
U.S.	387	21	676	37	751	41	0	0	0	0	1,814	100
Korea	30	2	558	36	932	60	0	0	31	2	1551	100
U.S.-Colombia												
U.S.	387	21	1231	68	149	8	0	0	47	3	1,814	100
Colombia	0	0	714	78	206	22	0	0	0	0	920	100
U.S.-Panama												
U.S.	387	21	1228	68	152	8	2	0	47	3	1,816	100
Panama	270	19	691	49	459	32	0	0	2	0	1,422	100

[1] The table contains a count of simple tariff lines (not trade weighted) at the tariff line level (the HS8-digit level for Colombia, Panama, and the U.S. and the HS10-digit level for Korea).

[2] In the case of U.S. tariff treatment to Panama, this includes two subdivided tariff lines designated as receiving special designation.

Source: USDA, Economic Research Service.

Table A2.4. Selected processed food, fish, and other U.S. agricultural exports to Korea

	U.S. exports[1]	Tariff	Phase-in	Competitors
	$ millions	*Percent*	*Years*	
Processed fruit and vegetables	112			
Frozen french fry potatoes	27	18	0	Canada
Prepared/preserved sweet corn	20	15	5	Thailand
Mixtures of nuts	11	45	0	China
Other	55			
Snack foods	85			
Prepared/preserved potato chips	13	20	5	China
Chocolate and chocolate confectionery, filled, less than 2 kg	9	8	5	EU
Confectionery and food preparations containing cocoa, not for retail sale	8	8	NA	EU
Chocolate and chocolate confectionery, not filled, less than 25 kg	9	8	5	EU
Corn chips and similar snacks	5	8	NA	China
Other	40			

Fruit and vegetable juices	40			
Grape juice	11	45	0	Chile, EU
Mixtures of fruit juices	7	50	10	
Frozen orange juice	5	54	0	Brazil, Israel
Other	16			
Coffee, roasted	18	29.5	5	Korea, EU, Japan, Switzerland
Fish products	293			
Frozen Alaska pollock roe	86	10	NA	Russia
Frozen Alaska pollock surimi (fish paste)	80	10	NA	ASEAN, China
Frozen cod, except fillets, livers, and roe	22	10	NA	Russia
Firsh meal fit for human consumption	12	20	NA	
Other	94			
Beverages	41			
Beverage waters	8	8	0	EU
Grape wines	11	15	0	EU, Chile, Australia
Other	22			
Tobacco	21			
Unmanufactured tobacco	21	20	10	Brazil, EU, India, Malawi, China

NA= not available. ASEAN = Association of Southeast Asian Nations.

[1] Average for 2007-09.

Source: USDA, Economic Research Service calculations using Tariff Schedules of Korea and USDA's BICO (bulk, intermediate, and consumer) database.

End Notes

[1] The term "free trade agreement" (FTA) is used generically in this publication to describe nearly all bilateral and regional trade agreements, including customs unions. The term "trade agreement" (TA) is used when referring to the U.S.-Korea Trade Agreement (KORUS). The correct term for the U.S.-Colombia and U.S.-Panama agreements is "Trade Promotion Agreement" (TPA). As with KORUS, we sometimes refer to them as "TAs." To our knowledge, there are no discernable differences between FTAs, TAs, and TPAs. Use of the three terms is simply to be consistent with the actual name given to an individual agreement.

[2] These include, by date of entry into force, Singapore (2004), Chile (2004), Australia (2005), Morocco (2006), El Salvador (2006), Honduras (2006), Nicaragua (2006), Guatemala (2006), Bahrain (2006), Dominican Republic (2007), Costa Rica (2009), Oman (2009), and Peru (2009).

[3] In the case of the U.S.-Korea TA, the Korean National Assembly also had not yet ratified the agreement as of March 2011.

[4] Percentages estimated by authors using the United Nations Commodity Trade Statistics Database (UN COMTRADE).

[5] It is for this reason that free trade agreements are still commonly referred to as regional trade agreements, or RTAs. They are also referred to as trade promotion agreements (TPAs) and reciprocal trade agreements (also RTAs).

[6] The 10 members of the Association of Southeast Asian Nations (ASEAN) are Brunei, Cambodia, Indonesia, Laos, Malaysia, Burma (Myanmar), the Philippines, Singapore, Thailand, and Vietnam.

[7] The Harmonized System is a universal product nomenclature used to classify tariffs. Products are categorized by chapters, headings, and subheadings. Each subheading is identified by a unique six-digit code (the first two digits identify the chapter, while the first four digits correspond to the heading).

[8] Unless otherwise indicated, we use the WTO definition of agriculture, which includes goods found in HS chapters 01 to 24, (minus chapter 03 and certain fisheries products) and parts of chapters 29, 33, 35, 38, 40, 41, 50, 51, 52, 53 (all nonfood products of agricultural origin).

[9] The amounts in these figures are based on the import figures reported by each country, which may differ from the amounts the United States reports as exports to these countries.

[10] Soybeans accounted for the majority of U.S. agricultural exports to China during this period (an average of over $5.5 billion per year). There was one competing ASEAN country, Burma; because its soybean exports to China totaled $9,200 in just one year, this trade was not counted as being competitive.

[11] The category includes products such as beverage bases; some snack foods; some fruit juice preparations; coffee whiteners; herbal tea mixes; some gelatin preparations; and many other processed foods, beverages, and food ingredients.

[12] For example, Korea charges a 50-percent tariff on oranges, a 40-percent tariff on beef, and a 25-percent tariff on frozen pork.

[13] Fabiosa et al. (2007) model a yearby-year scenario of the U.S.-Korea TA through 2016 and find a 19-percent expansion of U.S. beef exports by 2016. Although U.S. exports would still face a 30-percent tariff in 2016, the levy on competitors would be 40 percent.

[14] Fabiosa et al. (2007) estimate that partial liberalization of imports from the United States by 2016 would increase U.S. pork exports by 21 percent and poultry exports by 5.6 percent.

[15] This range was calculated by performing a systematic sensitivity analysis of the model with respect to two of its key parameters, the elasticities of substitution between domestic and imported varieties of goods and between different foreign suppliers of goods.

[16] Price bands serve to insulate producers and processors from trade competition when the world price for an imported good falls below a calculated reference price. Under the price band system, variable monthly duties, which may be positive or negative, are imposed on top of ad valorem tariffs to keep domestic prices within a predetermined range.

[17] These TRQs are in addition to those the United States created under the Uruguay Round Agreement on Agriculture.

INDEX

A

B

U

V

W

Y

Z